Service Bef

A Tribute to the Indian Military Academy Before and After Partition

CHARLES WRIGHT

RABY

First published in 2002
by Raby Books
The Coach House
Eggleston Hall
Eggleston
County Durham
DL12 0AG

British Library Cataloguing-in-Publication data
A catalogue record for this book is available from the British Library

ISBN 1-84410-006-5

Printed and bound in the UK by Alden Press, Oxford

Cover Illustration: Aerial photograph of Chetwode Building

This book is dedicated to:

Lt Gen. Thakur Mahadeo Singh DSO
First Indian Commandant of the
Indian Military Academy

Contents

Part Three

Part Four

Appendices

Acknowledgements

I WISH TO THANK Lt. General Amarjit Sandhu Commandant of the Indian Military Academy 1996–97, for his approval to publish this tribute to the Indian Military Academy and for the excellent article, The Cradle of Military Leadership being a summary of the activities of the IMA today, together with fine colour photographs showing the improvements that have taken place in the intervening years. The reader can thus look back on the past and forward to the future of this memorable institution.

I also wish to thank Sue Souter who has painstakingly read and corrected the proofs sent to her at Chantilly and has done a yeoman's service. Without her assistance this Tribute to the IMA could not have been successfully completed.

To Vera, my wife, who has not only proof read and corrected the scripts, but has given me wholehearted support in the venture at all times, I express my deepest gratitude and profound thanks.

Foreword

by
Lieutenant General Sir James Wilson, KBE, MC, DL

I AM DELIGHTED, and proud also, that Charles Wright should have asked me to write a short foreword to his book, *Service before Self*, about the Indian Military Academy. The IMA is one of India's most important national institutions; it has rendered great service to the country since its foundation in 1932.

Charles Wright's book covers a key period of the IMA's history from 1946, when it re-opened as an Academy to train regular officers only, until it had settled down after 1949 in its role on behalf of the reformed Indian Army after Partition. He deals with the basis of the Academy's training before partition was conceived and describes both the process of partition and the manner in which the IMA not only survived the ordeal, but became progressively larger and more significant.

I was privileged, as a very young officer, aged 25 or so, to play a full part in the IMA's development between 1946 and 1947. It was our aim to provide the best possible training for India's new regular officers and to hand over a flourishing Academy to the newly independent member of the Commonwealth. We tried hard and did our best; those who read Charles Wright's account will be able to judge for themselves the extent to which we were successful.

For my part, my memories of the IMA are exceptionally happy. I remember, above all, the friendliness of the Academy, the comradeship which existed between us all, and the determination to set and maintain only the highest standards. I have been lucky enough to revisit the IMA since on two occasions – in 1974 when I had the privilege, rare for an officer in a foreign Army, of addressing the assembled cadets in the Chetwode Hall, and in 1982 for the Academy's Fiftieth Anniversary. I saw enough on those two later visits to appreciate what a great institution the modern IMA has become. If those of my generation helped early on to lay sound foundations, we can, I hope, share just a little of India's justified pride in the present Academy.

India's armed services and her Army in particular, have served her well since Independence. Above all, as we tried to teach from the beginning, India's armed services have kept free from politics and served successive governments loyally and impartially. I have little doubt that in consequence democracy will continue to flourish in India, and that the IMA, by continuing to insist on sound principles will play its full part in the further development of a great country.

I wish Charles Wright's book every success; may it be widely read and its lesson of 'Service before Self' remembered and practised.

Lietenant General Sir James Wilson KBE, MC, DL
Adjutant, Indian Military Academy, 1945–1947

Author's Note

SERVICE BEFORE SELF has been compiled largely from extracts from the IMA Journals from 1946 to 1950, which include notable speeches made by Pandit Nehru, Mountbatten, Rajagopalachari, the first President of India, Auchinleck and many other dignitaties. It also includes numerous illustrations commemorating not only the notable events, but also the officers both British and Indian, who were so active in the handover of power at the time of Independence.

First and foremost I would like to acknowledge a great debt to Lt Gen. Sir James Wilson KBE, MC, DL, who has very kindly not only written the Foreword, but has also contributed a tribute to Brigadier A. B. Baltrop OBE, MC, the last British Commandant and a tribute to Lt Gen. S. P. Malhotra PVSM, who was the first Indian Adjutant of the IMA while he himself was the last British Adjutant.

Secondly, I would like to acknowledge Lt Gen. Malhotra's tribute to Maj. Gen. Thakur Mahadeo Singh DSO, who was the first Indian Commandant of the IMA and who was responsible for the smooth takeover from the British and for the formation of the Interservices Wing of the National Defence Academy.

I also wish to thank Lt Gen. M. Attiqur Rahman for his contribution entitled 'The Partition of India', describing the departure of the Mohammedan Officers, cadets and civilians, whose refugee camp he set up in the IMA compound, and a description of their hazardous journey to Pakistan by land and sea.

Finally I would like to thank Lt Gen. Harbakhsh Singh PVC for his contribution 'A Memorable Day at the IMA' describing a cadet prank that took place when he was a Gentleman Cadet, later becoming Deputy Commandant.

These contributions from officers who were my contemporaries at the IMA have brought back nostalgic memories of half a century ago. I do thank one and all for their very kind cooperation. These contributions have cemented together the extracts and photographs from the IMA Journals many of which I edited as Assistant Commandant (AEC) and Director of Studies. The compilation has been a labour of love and I trust it will give pleasure to many an ex-officer and Gentleman Cadet.

Charles Wright

Introduction

THE PURPOSE OF THIS BOOK is to pay tribute to the Indian Military Academy at the time of the handover of the British Command to the Indian Command.

The credit for the smooth handover must inevitably go to the outgoing Commandant Brigadier A. B. Baltrop OBE, MC and the incoming Commandant Brigadier Thakur Mahadeo Singh DSO, who both worked so tirelessly to ensure that this sensitive operation should go as smoothly as possible. They were ably assisted by the then Adjutant Major A. J. Wilson MC, of the Rifle Brigade. His liaison between the two Commandants was all important and due credit must be given to

The Main Gates.

his able handling of this delicate situation. Great credit also must be given to Major S. P. Malhotra, the first Indian Adjutant of the IMA.

Credit also must be given to all those who assisted in this process, notably the two British Deputy Commandants, namely Col R. S. Steed and later Col H. R. Power, who remained at the helm to the conclusion of the negotiations. These officers and Lt Col E. C. Gould, Assistant Commandant (RAEC), were largely responsible, with their assistants, for an operation that worked like clockwork. The Academy motto 'Service Before Self' exemplifies the tireless work of those who made the operation such a success.

When I arrived at the IMA in April 1946, partition had not been declared, for negotiations were going on in Delhi and no one at that time foresaw that it would be so imminent. True there had been demonstrations in many parts of India demanding freedom from British rule, notably in Calcutta, where the Sikh general, who had organised the Indian National Army in Burma to oppose the Indian Army forces on the frontiers of India and Burma, was being tried for treason and was imprisoned in the Red Fort.

These riots were, of course, anti-British, and feelings ran very high in Calcutta. It so happened that I, then in Shillong running the Eastern Command Educational Training Centre, received my posting orders to Dehra Dun. I had to travel from Shillong on the narrow gauge railway to Calcutta, from where I was to travel on to Dehra Dun on the main line a few days later.

Unfortunately my wife was in transit from Ranchi with our heavy luggage to Shillong, where we had expected to remain for some months. While I was staying at the Grand Hotel in transit, riots broke out in Calcutta. I witnessed plate glass shop windows in Chowringhee being smashed, shops looted and military trucks parked there burned. By this time there was a curfew and no one was allowed out of the Grand Hotel. However, three young officers seeing the trucks being set alight ran out and drove one remaining vehicle into the safety of the military car park opposite. For this the three were duly censured, but the authorities turned a blind eye on this heroic incident.

At this time militant crowds were not only lootings shops, but entering government offices, rampaging through buildings and throwing out files into the streets. I witnessed one such incident from the windows of the Grand Hotel, little realising that close by the Annex to the British Officers Club was being besieged by a violent mob. As there was a curfew at the time no one was allowed out of doors and consequently the residents including five officers' wives were barricaded indoors. The metal gates at the entrance hall had been locked, but the mob smashed them with a battering ram and entered the ground floor looting and breaking open cabinets and cases in their lust for revenge.

Major Murray Lewis (later Lt Col Lewis MBE) and one other officer in the Club were armed with revolvers and were prepared if necessary to open fire. The officers' wives were terrified and came to Murray Lewis, who advised them to lock themselves in the bathrooms at the back of the building. Unwilling to face 'a fate worse than death', they made him swear to shoot them rather than let the mob get them alive. Reluctantly Murray Lewis agreed and saw them locked in the bathrooms.

In the meantime, the mob having ransacked the ground floor began to mount the staircase, whereupon Murray Lewis and his companion fired two shots in the air. To his relief the mob turned tail and fled, only to foregather outside in the street and throw stones at the upper windows, smashing them before re-entering the building.

Suddenly there was an almighty bang and a blinding flash and the whole building shuddered and shook. It seemed that the end had come and Murray Lewis cocked his revolver ready to execute his duty and keep his promise to the officers' wives. But after a momentary respite the clouds burst following the thunder and lightning and the long prayed for monsoon with torrential sheets of rain flooding the streets had arrived.

In no time the street outside the Annex was clear of the thousands of demonstrators and the beleagured men and women inside the British Officer's Club Annex were safe.

Murray Lewis remarked after this terrifying incident 'Allah, Buddha and Vishnu and the minor gods were, it seems, on the side of the Christians'.

When I first heard this story from his lips, a cold shiver went down my spine, as it does as I relate it here. This is yet another example of Service Before Self.

When my wife and I ultimately left Calcutta, we were very fortunate for even worse riots were to follow at the time of Partition when blood flowed through the streets of Calcutta and daily dozens of cart loads of corpses were carried to the burial grounds as depicted in *The Times of India* with gruesome photographs. Not only in Calcutta, but also in

Delhi and above all in Lahore, terrible atrocities took place. But I must confine myself to Dehra Dun and the IMA.

I had not long settled at the Academy before there were the first rumblings of discontent in the locality. It was a complete shock to us at the IMA when we picked up the *Times of India* to read that Attlee had decided to grant Independence within six months and Mountbatten was given the onerous task of getting Mohd Ali Jinnah and Pandit Nehru to agree on how to divide the subcontinent with the least disruption. He was faced with a daunting task. Jinnah insisted on Partition, which Nehru was against, trying to preserve the comparative equilibrium attained by the British Government in preserving a state in which all communities could live in comparative peace. Furthermore, the Sikhs were demanding their share of the subcontinent, quite naturally, but Jinnah was firm and insisted upon the new State of Pakistan, ignoring the Sikh claim of a Sikh State lying between Pakistan in the North and India in the South. Feelings ran very high indeed and there were many minor riots, crowds marching through the city streets shouting 'Jai Hind'. These at first were fairly peaceful demonstrations, but many clashes took place. The greatest problem perhaps was not the safety of the Muslims or Hindus, but the survival of the Sikhs, whose territory lay roughly between the proposed boundaries of Pakistan and India.

Chetwode building.

Six months is no time in order to settle a dispute of such proportions, and as time passed Mountbatten had to decide the outcome. We all know what followed. The Sikhs were ignored, perhaps because they were in the minority and had no leader as powerful as Nehru or as Jinnah. Who was I to judge, but I favoured Nehru's view of a United India. After all for the last 100 years since the Mutiny in 1857, no great upheaval had taken place if one can overlook communal riots and the Jalalabad incident. Muslims, Hindus, Sikhs, Anglo-Indians and domiciled Europeans had all learned to live side by side, often being taught in the same schools and colleges and working in industry and commerce. Admittedly there were schools for Hindus, schools for Sikhs, schools for Muslims and schools for Anglo-Indians, such as the Lawrence Royal Military Schools, the Bishop Conton Schools and many others.

All this must be sacrificed for the desire for Partition, based largely on religious hatred, for as soon as Partition was declared all hell was let loose in cities, towns and villages. Religious hatred replaced religious tolerance, friends became enemies overnight.

Even worse was the fact that land became disputed, for the Muslims, Hindus and Sikhs had spread all over India, living in comparative peace, with occasional riots here and there. Now it was a question of religious rights. Some of those who lived South of the border had to move

Chetwode Hall.

North, and those North of the border had to move South, while the unfortunate Sikhs were sandwiched in between.

The Sikhs are noted to be a fine warlike race, carrying their kirpans as part of their religious rites, while for the most part Hindus and Muslims were unarmed. This in some cases caused fear and jealousy and resulted in many a riot.

Some wise men decided to exchange their properties, that is to exchange their land and property North of the border for land and property South of the border and vice versa. These changes took place between Hindus and Muslims for the most part, but they were in the minority. The vast majority had to decide to abandon their land and property and flee, either North or South. During these mass exoduses thousands were massacred as they attempted to emigrate.

In *Dehra Dun* itself during the height of the troubles we were told that about 100 a day were being killed. The worst trouble took place when refugees came down from Mussoorie. There is a half way halt where those coming down the one-way road await those coming up from Dehra Dun. Then the flow of traffic is reversed and goes up or down the one way restricted route. At this half way halt many refugees were killed. Likewise those travelling from Dehra Dun to Delhi were waylayed at the river crossing between Dehra Dun and Saharanpur, the bridge being damaged and passengers having to alight in order to cross the river and board a relief train on the other bank. Here again many deaths occurred.

I had been expecting a replacement officer from Delhi and when he failed to turn up at Dehra Dun I reported the matter. Three days later word came from HQ that he had been murdered in transit.

Security Measures

THE ACADEMY CEASED its normal functioning for three weeks during the height of the troubles. The officers and cadets were divided into three sections, one section to parade the town and collect the mail, if any, from the station, which had become a veritable fortress, harbouring refugees who wished to travel by rail. These included missionary families from Mussoorie and outlying districts who were accommodated in the waiting rooms for days on end, awaiting a train to transport them to safety. But the railway line had been cut and for a time no trains ran.

The second section was on guard duty in the IMA grounds, patrolling day and night, for some of the officers' bungalows abutted onto the semi-jungle, where there were no perimeter fences, as my house did. The third section were at rest, there being eight hour shifts.

At this time my first wife, Dulcie, was away visiting her mother, who had had a heart attack, and she was on the way back to Dehra Dun. I asked permission to go in one of the armoured trucks which patrolled the town, to see if any train had arrived or if any women were travelling. For two days I visited the station in vain, no trains were running and no women were allowed to travel. On the third day when I was growing more anxious the station master informed me that the telephone line had been cut and that no train was expected. There were others like me waiting anxiously on platforms, when the station master came to us and said the telephone lines had been repaired and a train was expected. When I asked if there were any women on board he said 'Yes'. So I waited impatiently awaiting the arrival of the train. It duly arrived and, lo and behold, there was Dulcie looking somewhat dishevelled. She was accompanied by a young servant her mother had insisted upon her taking from Ranchi. To my amazement the servant turned out to be a Muslim. He had survived the journey by travelling in my wife's coupé. There were no corridors on the Indian railways in those days because of dacoits. The carriage windows had wooden shutters, wire gauge shutters and window panes, all of which could only be opened from the inside.

I was naturally delighted that Dulcie had survived the journey, but anxious about the boy servant, who insisted upon going back to Ranchi. Reluctantly we let him go, which meant he had to travel in a third class compartment which accommodated dozens of passengers. It is nearly a 1000 mile journey with two nights on the train.

Apparently he had a frustrating journey for the train was searched from time to time for refugees. On approaching Calcutta two of his companions known to be Muslims were murdered and thrown out of the train. When he was questioned he said that he was a Hindu, and showed tattoo marks on his forearm 'M. K.' 'Mohd Khan', they cried 'No Mohan Khana'; he replied and they released him, and he lived to tell the story to my mother-in-law, Mrs Guise, on returning to Ranchi.

A number of the Indian AEC Officers and their families lived in Dehra Dun and they had to travel to and from the Academy each day.

This had become a risky business, for even military trucks were stopped in case the driver was a Muslim. I went to the Deputy Commandant and informed him I wanted all my officers and their wives accommodated within the IMA perimeter. He replied that there were no quarters available in the IMA compound. I then said 'Are you prepared to take the responsibility if one of my officers is murdered?' He was silent for a moment and then said 'I'll see what I can do'.

It so happened that there was a POW camp alongside the IMA compound. This camp had recently been vacated, the POWs (German and Italian) being released. Here it was decided to house all my officers and their families, and as a result there were no casualties.

In Delhi and Lahore terrible riots took place, dead bodies being left sometimes for hours in the midday sun before being collected, for fear of reprisals. Lahore was said to be the worst, for it was near the frontier and the death toll was probably never recorded, many refugees being massacred as they endeavoured to cross the border North or South as the case might be.

In Dehra Dun where there was military control, the cadets experienced their first taste of hostilities and better training they could hardly have ever had. They also observed the IMA motto – 'Service before Self'.

I have endeavoured to cover all the numerous activities of the cadets, whether they concerned military, academic or recreational issues. Many of these are illustrated, for photographs not only depict the activities concerned, but portray the very individuals who took part and excelled.

In the Appendices will be found a letter from Lt Gen. 'Turk' Rahman entitled *The Partition of India*, an article by Lt Gen. Harbakhsh Singh entitled *A Memorable Day at the IMA*, an illustrated article on the IMA Theatre, another entitled *Down to the Tons Valley in December* and one entitled *A Visit to Kashmir*. These, I trust, give a picture of the life of the cadet and his surroundings. It is all now history, but a glance back at the activities of 50 years ago may give the reader, young or old, a sense of pride in having served the Indian Military Academy.

Part One

The Indian Military Academy

Chetwode Hall

NAMED AFTER Field Marshall Lord Chetwode, Commander-in-Chief of the Indian Army at the time of the inauguration of the IMA is the central hall, where all the great assemblies take place apart from the Passing-out Parades. Here the Commandant addresses the Gentleman Cadets on their arrival and here they receive their 'pips' on being commissioned on the night of the Passing-out Parade, precisely at midnight.

The hall is magnificently panelled and there is a fine parquet flooring. The walls bear the Arms of the Earl of Willingdon and the Marques of Linlithgow, successive Viceroys of India.

Here too are laid up the banners of the former British Regiments handed over to General Thimayya when he was Commandant of the IMA after the successful conclusion of the Kashmir War.

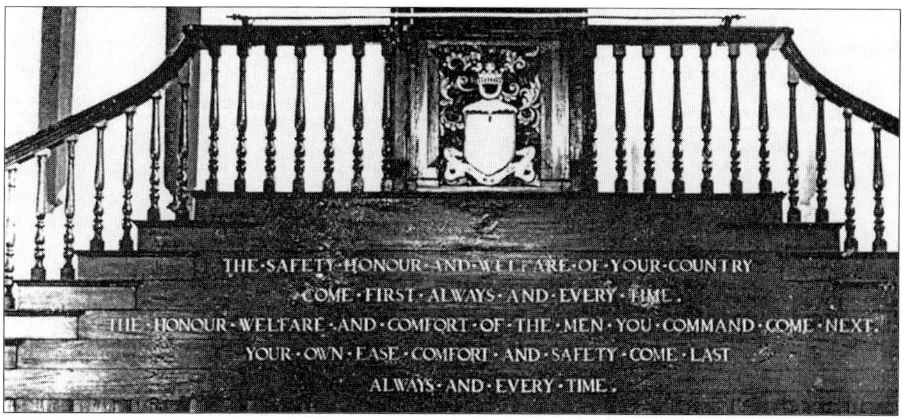

The dais, Chetwode Hall, Extract from Field Marshal Lord Chetwode's inaugural speech at the opening of the Indian Military Academy, 10 December 1932.

Here too are the Honours Boards commemorating those who fell in time of war, while the Awards & Decorations include such names as 2/Lieut P S Bhagat VC and Capt S. H. F. J. Manekshaw MC, the first Indian officer to become a Field Marshal.

In the Gallery above the Hall is the Museum, which contains the Memorabilia of the Academy from its inception, including the Sword of Honour presented to Lieut P. M. Lumsden (Killed in 1942) which I had the privilege to present to the Academy on behalf of his mother.

Every Cadet will remember above all perhaps the famous words of Field Marshall Lord Chetwode engraved in golden letters on the front of the dais:

THE SAFETY, HONOUR & WELFARE OF YOUR COUNTRY COME FIRST ALWAYS AND EVERY TIME:

THE HONOUR, WELFARE AND COMFORT OF THE MEN YOU COMMAND COME NEXT:

YOUR OWN EASE, COMFORT AND SAFETY COME LAST ALWAYS AND EVERY TIME.

It is these words that are imprinted on the hearts of every Gentleman Cadet and every officer who has had the honour to serve the Indian Military Academy.

Chetwode Hall.

The History of the Indian Military Academy

Plans for an Academy in India

THE PRESENT Indian Military Academy was founded on the sound principles of discipline, loyalty and respect.

Before the 1914–18 War, Indians were not eligible for King's Commissions in the Army. However, a link between the rank and file of the Officers was provided by the bestowal of Viceroy's Commissions on Indian Soldiers of outstanding merit.

In 1920 King's Commissions were bestowed on Indian gentlemen who passed a qualifying examination, which was held bi-annually in India, for entrance to the RMC Sandhurst or the RMA Woowich.

In addition to this Honorary King's Commissions were bestowed on VCOs with a distinguished record, but whose educational qualifications debarred them from equality with KCOs.

The Cadet's College, Indore

IN OCTOBER 1918 a Cadet College was opened at Indore. This was equivalent to an OTS training, and in the period of one year 30 Indian Gentlemen qualified for entrance to either Sandhurst or Woolwich, as Infantry or Cavalry Officers only, and received King's Commissions. Among these was the future C-in-C of the Indian Army, General Cariappa.

Indianisation

WITH THE INDIANISATION of the Indian Army, both Woolwich and Cranwell were opened to Indians, with the intention of forming Indian Artillery, Engineer and Air Units.

By 1934 no less than 179 Indians had passed out of Sandhurst.

The Skeen Committee

IN 1926 the Government of India suggested the founding of an 'Indian Sandhurst' to improve the standard and increase the supply of Indian Cadets. As a result the Skeen Committee, headed by the Chief of General Staff, Sir Andrew Skeen, as Chairman, was formed. This Committee reported in favour of an 'Indian Sandhurst' to be opened 'at the earliest by 1933' in order to advance the scheme of Indianisation in India itself. It also recommended the continuance of the allotment of vacancies at Sandhurst for Indians.

1931: a committee of experts was appointed under the Chairmanship of FM Sir Philip Chetwode, Commander-in-Chief in India, who recommended the establishment of a College by the end of 1932.

The Railway Staff Training College

A SERIOUS SET-BACK was caused by the World Slump, which, however, proved to be a blessing in disguise, for although sufficient funds were not forthcoming for building, it was as a result of the world financial crisis that the Railway Board had to abandon its project of opening the Railway Staff Training College at Dehra Dun, which had already been completed. Thus, by an agreement between the two Government Departments concerned the imposing buildings, which now comprise the Indian Military Academy, were handed over. It only remained to select suitable candidates to represent the first intake of Officer Cadets.

The Selection of Candidates

THE RULES for the regulation of admission by examination were published and in spite of the variety of subjects to be taken within two weeks 800 applications had been received for the 15 vacancies for 'open cadets'. Another 15 cadets were to be selected from Army Cadets, that is, those who were already in the Army, who held the rank of L/Naik or over and who possessed a first class Indian Army Certificate of Education. In this way, 30 cadets were selected bi-annually.

Courses were originally to be of 3 years duration, but this was reduced to 2½ years. The cost of the Course was estimated to be Rs. 10,755 of which the cadet's parent was to pay one third and the Government of India the remaining two thirds.

The Opening of the IMA

ON THE 1 October 1932 the Indian Military Academy opened at Dehra Dun, with Brigadier L. P. Collins DSO, OBE, ADC as its first Commandant.

The first intake consisted of 40 cadets – 15 'open cadets', 15 Army Cadets, plus 10 cadets from the State Forces.

On the first Inauguration Day, 10 December 1932, these cadets gave an exceptionally fine display of drill and turnout before HE the Commander-in-Chief, Sir Philip Chetwode, who took the salute. In the Course of his speech he uttered those famous words, which are now engraved in gold on the fine oak panelling in Chetwode Hall.

The six-monthly intake of 40 cadets continued until the full complement of 200 was reached. The IMA was officered at that time by 12 British Officers and one VCO.

The King Emperor's Cadetship

IN FEBRUARY 1933 the first award of the King Emperor's Cadetship was granted to Kanyha Lal Atal. This cadetship carried with it a remission of fees payable at the Academy to the extent of Rs. 2,120.

The Colours

10 APRIL 1933 was a great day in the annals of the History of the IMA for it marked the occasion when the first old colours – the colours of the 1/11 Sikh Regiment – were committed to the charge of the IMA, and were handed over to the two Senior Cadets who carried them to their place of honour in Chetwode Hall.

The IMA Colours

THE IMA COLOURS – Red and Grey – were chosen not only because of the Academy's close association with Sandhurst, whose colours are Red and White, but as the Editor of the first IMA Journal (published at the end of 1933) announced, 'because it represented honour and strength in their likeness to blood and steel'.

Many new innovations took place in 1933 and 1934. Among these were the following:

The Viceroy's Banner

THE VICEROY'S BANNER was presented to the Academy on 28 November 1933 by HE The Commander-in-chief, Sir Philip Chetwode, on the occasion of his first annual inspection, and was handed to the champion company.

New Buildings

BESIDES the new hospital, which was completed and received its first patients at the end of 1933, a number of other buildings were completed including the fine Swimming Bath, the Workshops and the Armoury. In addition the impressive main gates were installed to replace the original gates, the playing fields were greatly extended and Riding and Fencing were introduced.

One particular point of interest was that Mussoorie was placed 'in bounds' for week-end leave and was besieged by the grey-flannelled cadets.

Four Cadet Companies

IN 1934 a large increase in the numbers of cadets made it possible to start four Companies, as was originally intended.

Cadets Mess

ANOTHER INNOVATION was the opening of the new cadets Mess, which was adorned with numerous Big Game Trophies presented by the Sikh Pioneers and the coveted Viceroy's Banner, which hung over the chair of the Under Officer of the Champion Company.

King George V Banner

'ON 18 November' to quote the IMA Journal, 'HE the Viceroy handed into the keeping of the IMA 'for ever' the colours, corresponding to the colours carried by units of the Regular Army, and a banner presented by HM the King. The Colours included the King's Colour and the Regimental Colour. The Banner which was named 'King George V Banner', was to be held by the Champion Company each year in addition to the Viceroy's Banner.

'One thousand guests were present to watch the 'handing over' ceremony. The Commander-in-Chief was also present. The Colours were consecrated by the Rev. A. H. Broughton, Chaplain at Dehra Dun, and afterwards HE The Commander-in-Chief requested HE The Viceroy to make the presentations. The Commandant, Brigadier Collins, accepted the Colours and Banner, and asked HE The Viceroy to convey to HM The King the deep appreciation of the Academy. After a General Salute to the Colours, they were escorted to their resting place in Chetwode Hall by the Champion Company.

The Chetwode Coat of Arms

'AT THE SAME ceremony, HE The Commander-in-Chief, Field Marshall Sir Philip Chetwode, presented to the IMA a representation of his Coat of Arms beautifully carved in wood. This was placed in Chetwode Hall over the panels bearing the words of advice given to cadets by HE himself on the day that he inaugurated the IMA.'

The Science Laboratory

IN 1934 a new wing containing the Science laboratory and lecture hall and other rooms were added to Chetwode Building; the parade ground was increased to more than double its former size and four more tennis courts were constructed.

The Colours of the 2/2 Punjab Regiment

IN 1935 the IMA received the handsome gift of the old colours of the 2/2 Punjab Regiment, which were hung after an impressive parade, in Chetwode Hall close to the Colours of the 1/11 Sikh Regiment. At about this time another treasured gift, the 'Cameron Jat' Cup was presented to the IMA. This was to commemorate the association of the Cameron Highlanders with the Platoon of Jats attached to them from 1919–1934.

Other Presentations

AMONG OTHER memorable presentations were a magnificent tiger skin by Major C. G. Toogood DSO, 2nd (KEP) Gurkha Rifles and the Sword of King Nadir of Persia by Under-Officer B. K. M. Rana.

The Cyclone

'THE ACADEMY in May 1936', to quote the IMA Journal once more 'was hit by a cyclone, and the roof of the Swimming Pool was badly damaged, as well as many buildings belonging to the IMA Contractor.'

The New C-in-C and the New Commandant

1935 SAW NOT ONLY a new Commander-in-Chief, Sir Robert Cassels, who laid the foundations stone of the IMA Library, but also a new Commandant, Brigadier H. W. W. B. Kingsley DSO. The IMA at this time had as a cadet the famous Punjab hockey player Dara, who was flown to Berlin for the Olympic Games in time to help India win the World Championship.

Brigadier H. W. W. B. Kingsley CIE, DSO, was succeeded by Brigadier K. De. L. Young CIE, MC, ADC, who commanded the IMA from

1939 to 1942 and was awarded the CIE for his fine work at the Academy, when Brigadier J.K.Jones DSO took over command.

With the outbreak of War the Academy had to serve a somewhat different purpose, and from 1941 it was converted into an OTS producing both British and Indian Officers with an intake of approximately 1000 a year.

The last British Commandant to command the IMA was Brigadier A. B. Baltrop OBE, MC, who had the arduous task of converting the War time OTS into a peace time training centre, which task he successfully completed, and also saw the IMA through the dark days of communal unrest following Partition in August 1947.

On 1 November 1947 Brigadier Thakur Mahadeo Singh DSO became the first Indian Commandant of the IMA and to him fell the task of reorganising the Academy and forming the Armed Forces Academy of which he became the first Commandant, an honour which he thoroughly deserved.

Courses

COURSES WERE NORMALLY of two years duration, except for Ex-University Graduates, who have one year's training and approximately 200 to 250 Cadets were commissioned annually. Candidates are selected by various Selection Boards, who carry out selection on scientific methods with the aid of a psychiatrist and a psychologist. There is NO entrance examination.

Staff

THE IMA is commanded by a Brigadier. Under the Commandant is a Deputy Commandant, a GSO I, Assistant Commandant (IAEC) and an Officer-in-Charge of Administration. In addition to these appointments there are the following special posts: GSO II (Training-Org & Adm), GSO II (Field Training), Methods Officer (dealing with the Methods of Instruction), Adjutant, Weapon Training Officer, D & M Instructor, PT Officer, Pay and Accounts Officer, Quartermaster and Medical Officer. The remainder being officer instructors either on the military or academic side.

Objects of Training

OUR OBJECT is to ensure that each cadet shall acquire the mental, moral and physical attributes essential to his progressive and continued development as an officer of the regular forces, and that he shall also gain the basic military knowledge and educational background essential to all officers whatever their arm or branch of the service may be.

To this end, Cadets will:

(a) Be imbued with leadership qualities.

(b) Be given broad general basic education, both military and academic.

(c) Be trained to a high standard of physical fitness and endurance.

(d) Be given a high sense of duty, honour, purpose and service.

(e) Be made to realise the responsibilities of holding a commission in the regular forces.

Training

CHARACTER BUILDING and leadership training. In all activities – work, games, hobbies – we for ever hold our object in view and let it dominate the whole life and atmosphere of the Academy.

Leadership training is made implicit in every period of the programme and in all our activities both on and off Parade and we are constantly on the lookout for new methods of developing these qualities.

Leadership is also explicit in the syllabus, thus:

(a) Special training camps and exercises to develop powers of command, especially the qualities of initiative, physical and mental endurance, self-reliance and self discipline.

(b) Military Instructorship training, which develops self-confidence and personality.

Instruction in Military Subjects

BESIDES DRILL, for which there is a highly trained staff, the cadet's instruction covers a very wide field, including Weapon Training, Field Engineering, Organisation and Administration, Man Management, Radio Telephony, Intelligence and Security Training, Tactics and Military Writing and Military Law.

Academic Instruction

THE OBJECT of the academic training is to give the cadets an all-round background knowledge at university level, to cultivate in them a developed personality, dominated by reason and to inherit India's great cultural heritage. The main subjects taught are in English, which is the medium of instruction in the Academy, as cadets come from all parts of India and have many different mother tongues, World History, including Military History, Military Geography and Economic History, Mathematics, both Advanced and Elimentary, Science, including Physics and Chemistry, Current Affairs and Citizenship. There is also Hindustani School for those wishing to learn Hindustani, and Higher and Lower Standard Examinations are held regularly.

Methods of Instruction

THE VERY LATEST methods of instruction are employed at the IMA Lectures both on military and academic subjects are not dull dissertations, but alive with visual aids, sound aids, demonstrations, cloth models and sand models, all of which help to enhance the cadets enthusiasm to learn.

Training films are shown in the Cinema. Epidiascopes are installed in some lecture halls, and there is a wire-recorder of the latest manufacture employed for sound aids, for voice production etc. This latter is of great use in training cadets as public speakers. In addition cadets have to prepare and deliver lectures on a variety of topics and to run discussion groups.

Cadet's Companies

CADET COMPANIES consisting of approx 115 cadets, are named after famous battles in which the Indian Army had distinguished itself in the last war – Alamein, Sangro, Cassino, Imphal, Meiktila and Kohima.

Cadet Appointments

DURING the course of his training at the IMA each cadet has the opportunity of holding a responsible post ranging from Academy Under Officer to Coy Quartermaster Sergeant. The following Company Appointments are held by cadets:

Senior Under Officers, Junior Under Officers, CSM, CQMS. In this way cadets have opportunities of carrying out executive administrative duties.

Discipline

DISCIPLINE is the key note of training at the IMA – discipline on the parade ground, in the lecture hall, in the mess, discipline in mind and body, in turn-out and in cleanliness, is insisted upon at all times. It is founded on the individual's pride in being Indian, his pride in belonging to the Indian Military Academy, and his pride in himself and everything he does.

The strictest obedience to all orders and immediate and accurate compliance with any command they may be given is expected of the cadets. Their watchword is punctuality, their slogan comradeship in arms.

Its Situation

THE INDIAN MILITARY ACADEMY is situated approximately 2300 ft above sea level in the most delightful countryside, in the heart of Doon Valley, with the Shiwaliks dominating one side and the lofty Himalayas the other.

Its Climate

THE CLIMATE is exceptional, the cold weather lasting from November

– March, when the temperature drops at night to as low as a few degrees above freezing and yet the day temperature seldom drops below 55°. The maximum temperature in the hot weather seldom rises above 106°. The local hills are an unforgettable sight when the snow descends upon Mussoorie, which is only an hour's journey by road. May and June are the only really hot months, and from July to October the rains bring a vivid green to all plant life in the valley.

First Impressions

THE VISITOR's first impression of the IMA is indeed a happy one. Spacious lawns and flowering gardens demand attention. And in these delightful surroundings is found a flourishing community, a busy world, living under pleasant conditions.

Cadet's Quarters

THE CADET's quarters are well appointed, most cadets having a bed-sitting room with an adjoining bathroom, while spacious ante-rooms are provided for each company. These are comfortable lounges with sofas and easy chairs, radio sets, indoor games including billiards, darts and karam boards. Each ante-room is supplied with an abundance of literature in the form of daily newspapers, weekly, monthly and quarterly periodicals.

Special Amenities – Hobbies and Clubs

EVERY KIND of amenity is provided at the IMA. Apart from the splendid ante-rooms, there are excellent cadet's messes, a café decorated and furnished in pleasing colours, a flourishing canteen, a tailor and moochi's shop and a cinema. In addition to this, there is an active Dramatic Club with its own theatre and green-rooms. Here both English and Hindustani plays are performed, recent productions having been Shaw's *Arms and the Man* and Sheriff's *Journey's End, Mamoo Jan*, Tagore's *Chitra* and Sheridan's *Scheming Lieutenant.* Here too musical entertainments are staged and reviews, written acted and produced by Cadets. In addition there is the Riding Club, the Naturalist and Hiking Club, the Library, Current Affairs and Debating Club, the Arts and Crafts Club, the Music Club, the Bridge Club and the Camera Club.

Besides these many attractions the IMA provides every type of sport – Football, Hockey and Cricket, Athletics, Tennis, Squash and Badminton, Volley Ball and Basketball, Golf, Riding and Fencing, and last, but by no means least Swimming and Diving in a really fine swimming bath. Here every cadet is taught to swim, and here the experts play their water polo matches.

Chetwode Building

CHETWODE BUILDING is an impressive piece of architecture (see photograph). Here are to be found the main offices, the lecture halls, four fitted with epidiascopes and sound recording machines, discussion rooms, cloth-model rooms, Science Laboratory, an up-to-date Information Room and a very fine Library where cadets can find peace and quiet from the busy lecture halls.

Chetwode Hall

THE SHOW PIECE of Chetwode Building is Chetwode Hall named after the Commander-in-Chief who officially opened the Academy on 12 December 1932.

This hall is magnificent. Panelled in oak with a polished parquet flooring, its walls are adorned with the family crests and arms of Viceroys and Commanders-in-Chief, with trophies presented to the Academy by Maharajas and other great men, consisting of swords and spears and all the accoutrements of the wars of the past. In the gallery above will be found the museum bristling with modern arms of all types, show cases of medals and interesting souvenirs.

Honours and Distinctions

IN THE MAIN HALL the Honours Boards bearing the names of all the great men who have been trained at this Academy are a prominent feature. During its short life the IMA can boast of one VC, one George Cross, one George Medal, 3 DSOs, 15 MBEs, 54 MCs and many other honours, and an already formidable Roll of Honour. Here, too, high up, rest the Banners of great Indian Regiments (See Honours and Awards).

Its Historic Past

IN THIS HISTORIC HALL the cadets hear the first and last address from the Commandant, and here too from the rafters have echoed the voices of many of India's greatest servants from Field Marshall Sir Philip Chetwode, on Inauguration Day 1932, to the present great leaders of this country:

Lord Mountbatten of Burma
Shri Rajagopalachari
Pandit Jawaharlal Nehru
Sardar Vallabhai Patel
Sardar Baldev Singh
Mrs Vijaylakshmi Pandit
Gen. Cariappa the Commander-in-Chief
Admiral Parry Naval Commander-in-Chief

Little wonder that the cadet comes away with a determination to succeed, a will to uphold all the great traditions of this truly great institution, indelibly imprinted on his mind in those famous words of Field Marshall Sir Philip Chetwode, in his Inaugural Address, and now printed in gold letters on the rostrum from which so many great men have spoken since.

The Future of the IMA

IN JANUARY 1949 the Academy took on a new lease of life, becoming the Armed Forces Academy with two Wings:

(a) the Interservice Wing at Clement Town, which trains cadets between the ages of 15 and 17 for all three services, Army, Navy and Air Force, and

(b) The Military Wing, which continues the training for Army Cadets only as heretofore.

The Interservice Wing will have an intake of approximately 250 cadets, until a total strength of 750 is reached, while the Military Wing will be increased to a total of 900 cadets, there being a bi-annual intake of approximately 200 cadets.

Ultimately the Armed Forces Academy will become the National Defence Academy and will be situated at Kadakawasla, a few miles

The Senior Instructor. Lieut-Colonel Mahadeo Singh DSO,
2nd Punjab Regiment.

outside Poona. This National War Academy will train cadets for all three services, besides having Kadakawasla lake at the disposal of the naval cadets, a landing ground was constructed for Air Force Cadets.

When the National War Academy is completed is should be the finest institution of its kind in the World.

Roll of Honour

A/Capt.	Nawin Chandra	17 Dogra Regt	1941
A/Capt.	K. C. Medappa	12 FF Regt	1941
Lieut	R. H. Challis	I Artillery	1942
Lieut	R. M. Lumsden	I Artillery	1942
Lieut	Raghubir Singh Rawat	5 Mahratta LI	1942
2/Lieut	J. R. D. Mehta	I Armoured Corps	1942
Lieut	V. J. Chadda	2 Punjab Regt	1941
2/Lieut	R. Battacherjee	I Armoured Corps	1942
T/Capt.	Dil Mohd. Khan	15 Punjab Regt	1943
2/Lieut	A. G. Tomlinson	12 FF Regt	1943
T/Capt.	Ujagar Singh Dhillon	1 Punjab Regt	1943
2/Lieut	P. M. W. Whitehouse	13 FF Rifles	1943
Lieut	D. N. Patel	5 Mahratta LI	1943
Capt.	Amir Alan Ali	5 Mahratta LI	1943
Lieut	R. F. Loftus Tottenham	2 Gurkha Rifles	1944
A/Major	Surendra Nath Mahant MC	5 Mahratta LI	1943
T/Capt.	A. M. Palande	5 Mahratta LI	1941
Lieut	Jagit Singh	6 Raj. Rifles	1944
Lieut	G. K. Mehta	19 Hyderbad Regt	1942
Capt.	Diljit Singh	15 Punjab Regt	1943
Major	Risal Singh MC	9 Jat Regt	1944
Capt.	R. C. Evans	5 R. Gurkha Rifles	1944
Lieut	E. C. K. Wilson	14 Gurkha Rifles	1944
Major	A. J. V. Samuels MC	9 Gurkha Rifles	1944
T/Major	Ghulam Qadir MC	17 Dogra Regt	1944
Lieut	S. J. Morgan	I Armoured Corps	1944
Lieut	Sadhu Singh Padda	I Armoured Corps	1944
Lieut	Khanjar Zaman Tiwana	1 Punjab Regt	1941
Capt.	Gurbakhsh Singh Virk	I Armoured Corps	1945
Capt.	Ashraf Jan	I Armoured Corps	1945
Major	Amar Singh MC	12 FF Regt	1944
Lt Col	Sarbjit Singh Kalha DSO	1 Punjab Regt	1946

Awards and Decorations

The Victoria Cross

2/Lieut	P. S. Bhagat	Indian Engineers	1941

The Distinguished Service Order

Capt	T. Khanzada	11 Sikh Regt	1942
Capt.	S. K. Korla	10 Baluch Regt	1942
Lt Col	Sarbjit Singh Kalha	1 Punjab Regt	1944
George Medal			
T/Capt.	Sartaj Singh	I Artillery	1943

The MBE

Capt.	Mohammad Musa	13 FF Rifles	1942
Lieut	Apar Singh	ISC	1942
Major	Agya Singh	5 Mahratta LI	1943
Capt.	Guzlar Ahmed	10 Baluch Regt	1944
Capt.	Hari Chand Badhwar	I Armoured Corps	1946
Capt.	A. C. Iyappa	ISC	1946

The Military Cross

Capt.	Mohd Yusuf Khan	13 FF Rifles	1937
Capt.	Mohindar Singh	11 Sikh Regt	1940
T/Capt.	Taj Mohammad Khanzada	11 Sikh Regt	1940
T/Capt.	Amant Singh Pathania	13 FF Rifles	1941
T/Capt.	Mohammad Sadiq	11 Sikh Regt	1941
T/Capt.	Mohammad Sadiq	11 Sikh Regt, Bar	1942
Lieut	Sadiqullah Khan	13 FF Rifles	1941
Capt.	Ranbir Bakshi	I Artillery	1942
Capt.	S. H. F. J. Manekshaw	12 FF Regt	1942
Capt.	Balbir Singh	19 Hyderabad Regt	1943
Capt.	Gangaram Parab	19 Hyderabad Regt	1943
Major	M. A. Rahman	12 FF Regt	1944
T/Major	D. C. Misra	6 Raj. Rifles	1944
Capt.	Swarup Singh Kalaan	6 Raj. Rifles	1943
Major	Nand Lal Kapoor	6 Raj. Rifles	1943
T/Major	Surendra Nath Mahant	5 Mahratta LI	1944

Awards and Decorations

The Military Cross (continued)

T/Major	Kashmir Singh Katoch	13 FF Rifles	1944
T/Major	J. T. Satarvala	13 FF Rifles	1944
Lieut	S. P. Kapila	I Artillery	1943
T/Capt.	Mian Khan	6 Raj. Rifles	1943
T/Major	Pritam Singh	16 Punjab Regt	1943
Major	Risal Singh	9 Jat Regt	1944
A/Major	Harwant Singh	11 Sikh Regt	1944
Major	A. J. V. Samuels	9 Gurkha Rifles	1944
Lieut	T. R. Walton	12 FF Regt	1944
T/Major	H. S. Sandhu	12 FF Regt	1944
A/Capt.	Ujagar Singh	11 Sikh Regt	1944
Major	Budh Singh, MC & Bar	1 Punjab Regt	1943
T/Major	Ghulam Qadir	17 Dogra Regt	1944
T/Major	Gian Chand	1 Punjab Regt	1944
Lieut	G. L. Young-Western	6 Raj. Rifles	1945
Lieut	D. M. Mackie	8 Ghurka Rifles	1944
Capt.	Riazul Karim Khan	I Armoured Corps	1945
Capt.	Amar Singh	12 FF Regt	1944
Major	P. C. Gupta	12 FF Regt	1945

Mentioned in Despatches

T/Major	S. K. Korla	10 Baluch Regt	1942
Major	Kashmir Singh Katoch	13 FF Rifles	1941
T/Capt.	A. M. Palande	5 Mahratta LI	1941
Lieut	B. C. Kapur	I Artillery	1944
T/Major	Umrao Singh	I Armoured Corps	1944
Capt.	Dil Mohd Khan	15 Punjab Regt	1944
T/Major	Ghulam Qadir	17 Dogra Regt	1944
Lieut	Khanjar Zaman Tiwana	1 Punjab Regt	1941

Commendation Card

Capt.	T. P. Rajan	13 FF Rifles	1943

Auchinleck Battalion

AUCHINLECK BATTALION first took definite shape with the influx of cadets to the IMA on 18 February 1946. Besides its complement of officers who are listed elsewhere in this journal, the battalion is at present composed of 127 cadets who represent all provinces of India, save Sind, Assam and Orissa. Ninety-two cadets came from civilian life, seventeen are ex-members of the RIN, thirteen are from the Indian Land Forces or ex OTS cadets, four ex-RIAF and one is from an Indian State.

The Punjab has fifty-two representatives, Bombay twenty-three, Madras eighteen, the CP and Berar twelve, Bengal fourteen, the UP six and Delhi one. The Battalion may well lay claim to represent the whole of India.

At present it is organised in two Companies 'Y' and 'Z', both of which are sub-divided into three platoons. In August when about another three hundred cadets are expected to be absorbed into the battalion the organisation will be based upon four or five Companies each composed of three platoons.

Brigadier A. B. Baltrop, OBE, MC

THE IMA WAS FORTUNATE in having Brigadier Baltrop as its first post-war Commandant, and also incidentally as the last British holder of that appointment. He came to the IMA in 1944, when the establishment was still a war time OTS, there was no certainty when the IMA reverted in 1946 to its proper role of training regular Indian Officers that 'Groppi' would be selected to continue as Commandant. There was a great deal of talent in the Indian Army at that time, and any number of successful fighting Brigadiers available from either the Italian or the Burma campaigns. Wisely, Field Marshall Auchinleck, having visited the IMA in September 1945, decided that Baltrop had the right qualities to get the new IMA off on the right foot, with the advantage of hindsight, there could not have been a better selection.

'Groppi' owed his nickname to an alleged predilection for sticky cakes purchased from a well known Italian restaurant of that name in Cairo. He had fought in the Middle East in World War I and won a Military Cross there, serving with his regiment the 3rd Gurkhas. Between the wars he served mostly within his regiment, with a notable interlude of four years as a Staff Officer looking after the affairs of the State Forces. He learnt much in this appointment about India as a whole, and also how GHQ worked. When World War II came, Baltrop was too old to command a battalion on active service, and lacked the experience to be a Brigade commander. Instead he was appointed to command the Regimental Centre in Dehra Dun, and did so outstandingly from 1942–1944, when he became Commandant of the IMA.

Baltrop's forte was training, for which he had a special bent. He understood perfectly the need for motivation and insisted on modern

Commandant, Brigadier A. B. Barltrop OBE, MC, IA.

The Adjutant, IMA, Major A. J. Wilson MC, The Rifle Brigade.

efficient methods of instruction. In this sort of thinking the Commandant was well ahead of his time, and the IMA was unique in the way training was planned and organised. He would not tolerate bad instruction and rightly demanded perfection from his instructors, officers, warrant officers and NCOs. Importantly, he recognised the significance of the academic side of the Academy. In Ernest Gould, an exceptional Assistant Commandant and founder of the academic wing, he had exactly the right man to help develop the whole young officer, with brawn and brain in proper balance.

As his Adjutant, and effectively his Chief of Staff, I found him a delight to work for. Arriving in the morning, one would find in one's tray a string of notes, scribbled in the Commander's hand, all requiring swift action. He left one alone to solve the problems he posed, and one only did so by involving immediately the real professionals on the staff who could develop a sensible answer. It was a stimulating atmosphere in which to work, and people grew in stature as they found new ideas welcomed and initiative encouraged. Baltrop was not a politician, though he certainly possessed political understanding. He never thought in terms of a divided India, for such was not his mandate or the way he had been trained to think. He found partition hard to bear, and, after August 1947, quickly decided on retirement. He welcomed his successor Brigadier (later General) Mahadeo Singh, who had previously been an outstanding Senior Instructor and was plainly the right man to carry the IMA forward.

Altogether Baltrop, courteous, kind, but determined to have only the best for the Academy, was just the right first Commandant for the post-war IMA. His wife, Marjorie, complemented him perfectly. They entertained generously and well, setting standards of civilised behaviour for all of us to follow. I was fortunate and privileged to work closely with him, the IMA was a highlight for my whole career, as it probably was also for very many others lucky enough to be at Dehra Dun between 1945 and 1947.

James Wilson
Lieutenant General
(Adjutant, IMA, 1945–47)

Commandant and Officers, Indian Military Academy 1946.

The Staff, 1946

- The Commandant
  - Adjutant
    - Deputy Commandant
      - SI
        - Military
        - Training
        - Staff
        - Field Training
        - Weapon Training
        - Physical Training
        - Driving and Maintenance
      - GSOI
      - Methods Officer
    - OC Auchinleck Battalion
    - Assistant Commandant RAEC
    - Office i/c Administration

Headquarters Indian Military Academy

Commandant: Brigaider A. B. Barltrop OBE, MC, IA.
Deputy Commandant and Colonel R. S. Steed, IA March to November 1946.
Chief Instructor: Colonel H. R. Power, IA From November 1946.
Adjutant: Major A. J. Wilson MC, The Rifle Brigade.

Training Staff

Senior Instructor: LT-Col Mahadeo Singh DSO 2nd Punjab Regiment.
GSO I. (Training Plans): Lt-Col W. R. Holman MC Royal Artillery.
Methods Officer: Major L. D. Gates, The Frontier Force Rifles.
Assistant Methods Officer: Captain B. V. Pilkington, 16th Punjab Regiment.
Assistant to Senior Instructor: Captain J. C. Jackson, REME.
Weapon Training Officer: Major P. K. Pisal, The Mahratta Light Infantry.
PT Officer: Captain R. H. D. Graveston, The Rajputana Rifles.
MT Officer: Captain J. D. Elliott, The Mahratta Light Infantry.
Instructor Class 'B' i/c Training Team: Major P. L. Stubbs MC, 2nd Gurkha Rifles.
Instructors Class 'C' Training Team: Captain H. B. Gray Royal Artillery.
Captain K. C. Parry MC, Royal Engineers.
Captain A. F. Downie, Royal Artillery, Captain I. S. Gill MC, Royal Engineers.

Academic Staff

Assistant Commandant (RAEC) Lt-Col E. C. Gould, RAEC.
Instructors Class 'B' (RAEC) Major C. H. E. Wright, RAEC.
Major K. D. Hiranandani, The Dogra Regiment.
Major Y. R. Puri, RIASC.
Instructors Class 'C' (RAEC) Captain P. G. B. Giles, RAEC.
Captain A. J. Bryan, RAEC.
Captain J. G. MacDonald, The Green Howards.
Captain S. K. Jha, The Sikh Regiment.
Captain D. G. Washtell, Intelligence Corps.
Captain B. M. Siddiqi, Intelligence Corps (India).
Captain S. J. Talibuddin, RIASC.
Captain P. Gorb, RAEC.
Captain A. N. Chatterji, The Frontier Force Rifles.
Captain J. S. Banerjee, Intelligence Corps (India).
Captain A. H. Hughes, RIASC.

Administrative Staff

Officer i/c Administration: Major W. D. Bevan, The Suffolk Regiment.
Welfare and Assistant Administrative Officer: Captain R. G. Price, Indian Armoured Corps.
Pay and Accounts Officer: Captain A. J. Caldicutt, SLQM, IA.
Quartermaster: Lieut. H. F. Edgerton, SLQM, IA.
Medical Officer: Captain R. M. Livingstone, RAMC.
Assistant Medical Officer: Lieut. A. V. Barker MBE, IAMC.
Matron: Miss L. Lyall MBE.

Auchinleck Battalion, Indian Military Academy

Commanding Officer: Lt-Col L. T. Firbank OBE, The Rajput Regiment
Adjutant: Captain M. G. Canning, Coldsteam Guards.

'A' Company

Major A. C. Iyappa MBE, Indian Signal Corps.
Captain M. Taskin-ud-din, 8th Punjab Regiment.
Captain R. J. Bobbett, Irish Guards.
Captain N. L. Singal, The Jat Regiment.
Captain R. C. Heape, Indian Armoured Corps.

'B' Company

Major T. R. Johnson, The Frontier Force Regiment.
Captain S. G. Mahdi MC, 15th Punjab Regiment.
Captain J. R. A. MacMullen MC, Irish Guards.
Captain Pritpal Singh, 5th Probyn's Horse.

'C' Company

Major K. Zorawar Singh MC, Central Indian Horse.
Captain T. D. Joshi, The Dumoan Regiment.
Captain J. W. Bell, Royal Armoured Corps.
Captain C. M. Sahani, KGVs O. Bengal S & M.

Major M. A. Rahman, MC, The Frontier Force Regt.
Captain Tikka Khan, Royal Indian Artillery.
Captain D. B. Harley, 2nd Gurkha Rifles.
Captain A. K. Naidu, RIASC.
Captain Dildar Singh, The Kamoan Regiment.

Editorial

June 1946

FROM FEBRUARY of this year, 1946, the IMA ceased to train men for Emergency Commissions and reverted to its former peacetime task of preparing exclusively Indian cadets for a professional career as regular officers of the Indian Army.

The IMA a truly national Institution, is pre-eminently and proudly Indian. Its cadets are drawn from all over India, they are united under the banner of patriotic service, they are fit in mind and body and devoted to the honourable task of maintaining and improving the lustre and glory of the Indian Army. In the IMA India can see a microcosm of itself – a microcosm in which are generated the ideals, disciplines and controls and moral, mental and physical energies which, streaming out into national life can refine, strengthen, amplify and inspire it. On 19 January we were honoured by a visit of HE the Commander-in-Chief, General Sir Claude Auchinleck who took the Passing Out Parade of 'B' Company.

The clear and illuminating address of Dr A. N. Jha, Vice-Chancellor of Allahabad University, on the future War Memorial Academy to be built at Poona, at once imparted to us a sense of modesty over our present accommodation, and a tingle of elation at the knowledge that we are now creating the legacy of tradition which the new Academy will inherit.

The article by Marjor A. J. Wilson MC, on the future of armoured forces in the current issue of this Journal is a most competent follow up of Major-General Boucher's excellent lecture on Airborne Forces and will probably cause even more cadets to envisage the sky as the only natural limit upon their military ambitions.

We were honoured by a visit from Lieut-General Sir A. R. Goodwin-Austin CB, OBE, MC, who took the Passing Out Parade of 'C' Company on 9 February. A review of the first term's progress and activities must give satisfaction to both staff and cadets alike. Formless and directionless beads of individual life have coalesced, become canalised and moved upstream on the currents of training, discipline and communal living, bubbled up into numerous clubs and eddied into little identifiable pools of personality and character. Strong tides of energy and activity are moving on the waters of the IMA, and the sparkle of sun and life is in and on them. Next term we shall welcome the second batch of peacetime cadets and by August our present juniors will be knowledgeable and fully fledged veterans.

Commandant's Opening Address

3rd Course – 25 January 1947

Introduction

GENTLEMEN, I extended to each one of you a warm welcome to the Indian Military Academy and I hope your time here will be as easy as it will be profitable.

Indian Military Academy

YOU HAVE already been told something of the history of the IMA and it only remains for me to impress on you that we are all very proud of it and of our traditions. These traditions have been built up by staff and cadets over the past fourteen years, and I may add that the large number of British and Indian cadets who were commissioned during the war years have played their full part in this process.

We shall expect you to play your full part too, and we shall expect you to be loyal to these traditions and to live up to the very high standard that we have set as our goal.

National Institution

THE IMA as its name implies, is a truly Indian National Institution and I am confident that, as such, you will become very proud of it. It follows from this that the mainsprings of our inspiration come from India's great cultural heritage and tradition ranging over 6,000 years and more. We want you cadets to be enthusiastic students of your country's culture, literature, art and music – all these and all that Indian civilisation in its finest manifestations stands for. We want to produce officers with unshakeable loyalty and faith in their country – for patriotism at its best is vital to our existence as a National Institution. But at the same time we must relate this culture to those of the other civilisations of the world and we must remember that the IMA is a university whose object is to illuminate the mind, lay world knowledge before it and cultivate above all a reasoned approach to life. Clear reasoning calmness in decision, a capacity for objective thought – these are the marks of a good education and are universally valid. I shall have more to say on this subject later when I deal with the academic side.

The Future of the IMA and Our Aim

WHEN THE buildings for the National War Academy are completed, the staff and cadets together with the traditions of the IMA will move to the new site. Thus the NWA will evolve physically from the IMA and it therefore follows that we staff and cadets here now are laying its foundations.

Our aim is to make the IMA the finest, most modern and up-to-date training establishment in the world, so that the NWA will have a flying start. Therefore we have a weighty responsibility. The goal I set before you is a 100 p. c. standard in everything we do – our training, our administration, our manners, our tone and reputation. Always hold this ideal before you.

Object of the Course

NOW LET ME tell you about the object of the course. Our object is to produce officers with all the many qualities of leadership and with a broad outlook on the world and military affairs. Also to give you basic military knowledge and an educational background. In fact, we shall give you the foundation on which to base your progressive and continued development of an officer of the regular forces.

Modern Methods

I AM SAFE in saying that nowhere could you find more modern methods of teaching.

The same applies to our system of Progress Reporting, that is your methods of recording your progress. You will be told about this by your officers. All I will say here is that our system is designed to help you by pointing out your weakness and by giving you advice as to how you can rectify them. By the way, you must learn to take correction or criticism in the right spirit – you will have a miserable life in the army if you do not.

Relegation and Withdrawal

I FEEL IT IS ONLY FAIR for me to tell you that you would be wrong if you thought you were all certain of getting your commissions. Those of you who do not make satisfactory progress will be either:

(a) Relegated to a later course for further instruction

or

(b) Withdrawn from the Academy.

You will be kept informed of your progress.

Now please don't think that I mention relegations and withdrawals as a threat. That is not the system on which we work here – far from it. It would both be dishonest to India and contrary to the interests of Indianisation of the army to commission cadets who do not come up to the required standard. It is the task of the IMA to build up a hard core of good officers. Upon the standard of officers commissioned from this Academy will depend in future the safety of India as well as the lives of her soldiers. The ultimate effect over the course of years of the acceptance of low standard at the IMA would be to reduce the high prestige and efficiency of the present Indian Army to that of a third class power.

But India wants a large number of officers and our subject is to turn as many of you as we can into officers.

Discipline

I TAKE IT that you all know what discipline means, and that you are all agreed that an army without a high standard of discipline is a danger to everyone concerned and a disgrace to a nation.

You are being trained to be officers. An officer must have a standard of discipline much higher than that which he expects from his men. The IMA is an officer-training establishment and therefore our discipline must be the finest in India. But what kind of discipline do we want here? And how is it maintained? Do we maintain it by fear of punishment? Certainly not. Discipline maintained in this way is the wrong kind of discipline.

We have the right kind of discipline here – that founded on your pride in being an Indian, your pride in belonging to the Indian Military Academy, and your pride in yourself and in everything you do.

Drill is the bedrock of discipline, allied with first class turnout at all times, by turnout I mean your bodily cleanliness, your spotless uniform, mufti and games clothes too, your smart appearance. So we expect from you first class turnout at all times, and I impress on you that there is only one kind of drill whether on the parade ground or elsewhere and that is first class drill. Whenever you drill put all you know into it. There is only one way of doing things and that is the correct way. Apply this to everything.

The same applies off parade, when you are walking about by yourself in the Academy grounds or outside. Never slouch about, with your hands in your pockets, your eyes on the ground, it is just on those occasions that we of the Academy are judged. And rightly so. Instead, march about smartly, alert, observant, eyes off the ground, inquisitively looking about you, well turned out, and punctilious in your saluting. Move about as if you had something to be proud of. And you certainly have.

All of us here – staff and cadets – take a great and justifiable pride in the IMA and we of the staff take pride in our cadets. I am confident that you too have great pride in having had the good fortune to belong here. Learn not to take things for granted. From time to time think of all the hard work that has been done over the past fourteen years in organising the Academy – and particularly in the year 1946.

Orders

WE EXPECT from you strict obedience to all orders and immediate and accurate compliance with any command that may be given you. Take pride in the exact carrying out of orders. You will find that one of our watchwords is PUNCTUALITY. Cultivate the habit of always arriving on time and let this habit remain with you throughout your life. Punctuality is a virtue. And so is TIDINESS – tidiness of your room, your work table and everything else.

There are certain things here that are just not done. You will learn these from the Seniors. It is not done to be badly turned out, to be slovenly, to have your hands in your pockets, to ride a bicycle after lighting-up time without a light and so on. If you do such things as this, not only will you be letting down the name of the Academy, but also you will meet with the disapproval of your brother cadets.

Academic

AS I SAID EARLIER, the IMA is a university and a university where only the highest standards of mental efficiency and achievement are wanted and recognised. Being a university, its range of knowledge is universal. While it is essential for you to be the inheritors and the torch-bearers of the great cultural heritage which thousands of years of Indian thought and activity have provided for you, it is equally essential that, as educated men, your knowledge should range over the major contributions to art, science, literature and the history of mankind. You will follow courses here designed to illuminate your minds, enlarge your sympathies and strengthen your judgement – courses which, in general scope and breadth, are unparalleled in any other institution in the world.

You must not expect to be spoon-fed here. In academic subjects as well as others, you will be expected to seek out knowledge for yourself, to make contributions to thought in the classroom, to be active and not passive.

The supreme object of our academic courses is to cultivate in you a developed personality, dominated by reason. Let me repeat what I said before, clear reasoning, calmness in decision, objectivity in thought – these characterize the educated man of all times and climes. Unless you have these virtues, you will certainly not become good officers. You will be pleased to hear that your academic work is not merely theorising, it is also doing. The civic lessons you learn here, you will have a chance of putting into practice in the neighbouring village of Rangarwalla. You all wish India well, here you will have every chance of doing some practical good for your countrymen. Finally, while I'm on the academic side of the IMA, the answers we shall seek from you will be largely concerned with the question of WHY and not of WHAT. Reason is more important than memory.

Games and Fitness

YOU WILL FIND ample scope at the Academy to play games and to learn how to organise them. Games play an important part in the life of an army officer, and troops rightly expect their officers to take an interest in their games. Skilled performance is not given to everybody and is in no way essential – but you should learn to take an interest in the efforts of your own unit and submit even if you cannot play yourself. I should like to take this opportunity of stressing the need for hardness and physical fitness in an officer – need not be an athlete, but he must be hard and fit and capable of higher standards of endurance than any of his own troops. The Indian soldier's standards in this respect are very high and you yourselves will have to be extremely fit, hard and determined, if you are to live up to the standards he will expect of you.

Clubs, Private Study, Cinema

DURING THE PAST YEAR the cadets, with the help of their officers, have organised various clubs such as Nature Study, Hiking, Shikar, Photography, Music, Debating Society and so on. There are seventeen clubs in all. It is important that an officer should have a hobby of some sort. If you already have a hobby, join the club concerned. If you have not, here is your chance to acquire one. But you will not be forced to join a club. They are entirely voluntary.

If you are to be successful you must make full use of the Private Study period, and to do this you must plan them carefully. Go to the cinema by all means, but don't get the cinema-going-habit – we don't want to produce film fans. I advise you only to see the worthwhile films the good films. Pick and choose, and the same applies to your reading too. Only read worthwhile books.

Editorial

December 1946

It must be gratifying to Indian public opinion at large and to the IMA in particular, that during the same year as the Constituent Assembly was convened to accelerate India's march to sovereignty, the first post-war course for regular commissions resulted in the accretion to the army of seventy-three fit, enthusiastic and well trained young Indian officers. The poise, balance and effective influence of the legislature of any government depends largely upon the character of its executive servants. It is with pride that the IMA bequeathes these disciplined and industrious young men of good-will to the nation. If a nation can be judged by the quality of its citizens, the IMA can be proud of its contribution to the future greatness of India. All those factors which go to make a country great, India possesses in profusion. Geographically, she is a natural link between East and West, especially in these days of air travel. Her immense and divine cultural heritage has been the delight and tutor of European and Asiatic alike. India shows every likelihood of becoming the largest group under one political system ever known to the world, in natural and potential resources, both industrial and agricultural, this subcontinent should with time stand comparison with Russia and the USA. In two modern wars, the quality of India's armed forces has excited the admirations of its allies and the fear of its enemies. The eyes of all Asia are focussed upon India as the guide to a freer, better and more abundant way of living. Nothing can stay India's forward march except herself, nothing can come between her and her high mission, except the difference lamentably existing between her own sons. At no time in history did India stand in greater need of wise, balanced and statesmanlike leaders than she does today. It is in no spirit of vain boasting, but rather in a spirit of humble thankfulness, that the claim is asserted that the Indian Military Academy has produced and continues, as its sole function, to produce leaders, the type of which India stands in sore need. Young men patriotic in the highest sense, who have been trained to put their country first, who not only have a vision of its greatness, but also are prepared to put in the hard work and solid effort which will enable their vision to become reality, young men in whom reason is dominant, judgement impartial, initiative developed, who seek not to avoid, but to shoulder greater and greater responsibilities, young men who are determined that their country shall not only attain its freedom, but also be able to defend and maintain it – these are leaders which the IMA develops and hands on as the highest possible gift, to the nation that gave them birth.

Spontaneity

WE LIKE OUR CADETS to be spontaneous. Don't be afraid to speak up. Do not give the answer calculated to please. Be frank and forthcoming. But beware of making stupid suggestions or stupid criticisms, just for the sake of it.

Politics

AN ARMY can have no politics, it is the servant of the people and must support whatever government is in power. Any army officer may hold whatever political opinions he likes, but he must not allow politics to affect his loyalty to his service or to the government in power.

Conclusion

IN CONCLUSION, gentlemen, let me set before you the ideal of SERVICE, which means 'helping to preserve or to obtain the well-being, the happiness and the enlightenment of *other* people'. Let your own ease and comfort come after this and be subordinate to it. In the army you will have a fine opportunity of service and unselfishness. Here at the

IMA you will learn the meaning of service to others. You will learn too that the only worthwhile happiness is that obtained from the very pleasant feeling of a job well done. There is no other kind of real happiness. Not everyone realises this. Always remember that you are

The Commander-in-Chief, Field Marshal Sir Claude J. E. Auchinteck GCB, GCIE, CSI, DSO, OBE, ADC.

making the army your profession, that you are going to be professional soldiers.

So get down to it and take full advantage of your time at this Academy. Here you will learn the code of the army, which is good manners, courtesy and comradeship. It is here that we lay the foundations of your military career – more than that – mould your character, so that nurtured in the atmosphere of the Academy and its traditions, you will not only be an efficient officer, but a man who has acquired a set of ideals, which will stay with you for ever.

I will end by reading to you our motto, which I hope will be the guide for you throughout your service.

The highlight of the past term was the visit of His Excellency the Commander-in-Chief. This visit marked the consummation of hope of the seventy-three cadets who passed out after a year of strenuous and high endeavour, it included a general inspection of all activities – military academic, club and sport of the IMA. The passing-out parade, the central purpose of the visit, was faultless in detail and magnificent in general aspect. It made it easy to understand the statement of an experienced officer – drill is essentially something spiritual.

The final after dinner address of Field Marshall Sir Claude Auchinleck penetrated with its sincerity, earnestness and spirit of close fellowship into the minds and hearts of all officers and cadets who were privileged to hear it – the aptest conclusion to the life of a cadet, an inspiration to the young officer embarking on a new career.

Amongst those in His Excellency The Commander-in-Chief's party were Air Marshall H. S. P. Walmsley CB, CBE, MC, DFC, Air Officer Commanding in India, Vice-Admiral Miles, Flag Officer Commanding, Royal Indian Navy and Major-General D. C. Hawthorn CB, DSO, Director of Military Training.

Visit of the Vice-President and Home Member

ON THE 25 MAY the IMA had the honour and distinction of a visit and speech by both the Vice-President of the present government Pandit Nehru and of the Home Member Sardar Patel. Since unfortunately the complete speech of Pandit Nehru is not available, we must perforce limit ourselves to his main observations.

Both staff and cadets were delighted to find that the Vice-President in spite of his illimitable responsibilities of State and his close packed daily routine, had found time to read up all the information on the life and objects of training of the IMA. He affirmed his full-hearted approval of all the objects of the IMA and added that if our achievements rose to the level of our endeavours they could not be improved upon. This entirely unsolicited testimonial from a great Indian leader upon our efforts to produce leaders for the Indian army, was undoubtedly a high compliment.

Pandit Nehru referred to the lustre which the exploits and campaigns of Indian soldiers in the last war and in former wars, had added to the glory of Indian arms and to the necessity of maintaining and, if possible, surpassing the standards hitherto achieved. What is an army? An army is an instrument of the government. What is a government? A government is the servant and representative of the people. The army likewise belonged to the people, was the servant of the people and should be integrated with the people. The army was not something apart from, distinct from or superior to the people. It was a limb of the State, organically joined to the people. The people should not only feel affection and pride for their army, they should know that the army is of them, one with them, their own.

RSM L. McGarrity, Irish Guards.

Sudebar Major Hoshair Singh Gurung, 3rd Gurkha Rifles.

Jawaharlal Nehru went on to say that an army should not always be looking backward. History showed that new weapons, new developments in techniques had usually brought victory to their users and exploiters. We are moving in an atomic age, the army must have its branches of scientific research and discovery if it were to keep up with the rapidly developing modern world. India had much leeway to make up. But it had to do so within the framework of its own traditions. A nation could not thrive on a borrowed culture and way of life. If it attempted to do so, it would find itself rootless. National development must be in an organic link between past, present and future. India must progress in her own way, handing on the best of its traditions, discarding those which burdened and retarded its forward march.

The most serious note of the speech was struck when Pandit Nehru referred his audience to the times through which they were living. The future was not going to be easy, freedom could be won through struggle, it could only be maintained through vigilance and sacrifice. Great movements could be started by men, but once they had gained momentum, they followed a course which their initiators could not always predict. Events contain in themselves a dynamism. Dynamic forces were now at work in India. Willynilly, people were being rushed along by the cataract of events. If people wanted a quiet life with security and safety first as their watchwords, they should have chosen to be born 100 years ago. The cadets in the IMA were so far sheltered. While they should look to the future with confidence, they must at the same time envisage it as calling forth all the powers of will, determination, courage and adaptability which transitional periods of history have from the earliest struggles of mankind demanded.

Random Notes

AFTER MANY YEARS of devoted service, Miss L. Lyall, MBE, the matron of the IMA Hospital, is shortly to leave the IMA. She will be greatly missed by staff and cadets alike. We offer our sincerest good wishes for her future happiness with Colonel W. A. Asher, RAEC.

Sword of Honour, 1946

B. P. Bhalla
United Provinces
Senior Under Officer
Cadet Company Commander
D Company
Represented IMA at: Hockey, Lawn Tennis, Rugby Football
President of Hindustani Majlis
Founder and President of Shakespeare Circle

Silver Medal, 1946
Cadet Battalion Commander

K. K. Kaul
Kashmir
Senior Under Officer
Secretary, Hindustani Majlis
Indian Armoured Corps

Our congratulations go to GC Bhalla and GC K. K. Kaul who, for outstanding merit over the whole ten months of their cadetships, were awarded the Sword of Honour and the Silver Medal respectively.

The successes of GC S. W. Burrett and GC E. Thomas in the Dehra Dun Olympic Games are worthy of special mention. Burrett, having won the mile race, proceeded to win the nine-mile marathon in the record time of 51 mins. 9 secs. Thomas won the trophy for the best athlete, being first in the broad and high jumps, and in putting the shot, and second in throwing the javelin.

The high spot of the earlier part of the term was the visit of Major General D. C. Hawthorn CB, DSO, Director of Military Training who took the salute at a Battalion Parade on 21 November 1946 and inspected field and academic training.

Auchinleck Battalion Notes

BEFORE WE SUMMARIZE this busy and successful term we must say goodbye to Lieut-Colonel L. T. Firbank, OBE, Commander of Auchinleck Battalion, who leaves after one year at the IMA, to take up the appointment of Inspector of Physical Training at GHQ. We wish him the very best of luck for the future.

The Christmas vacation ended on 20 January 1947 and the GCs of Auchinleck Battalion returned to find that a certain amount of reorganising had taken place during the break to receive the cadets of the Third course who brought the total numbers up to 558. An additional Company 'E' Company, came into being under the Command of Major G. E. A. Beale of the Frontier Force Rifles and the Indian Parachute Regiment.

This Company occupied the hutted quarters on the west wing of the playing fields, together with 'A' and 'C' Companies. 'D' Company, the Champion Company, moved into Collins Block, while 'B', the runners up, remained in Kingsley block.

A number of changes of officer appointments within Auchinleck Battalion occurred. Captain Pritpal Singh, 5th Probyns Horse, IAC was appointed Adjutant in place of Captain M. G. Canning, Coldstream Guards, appointed GSO III (Adjutant to the Senior Instructor) HQ, IMA, on 10 March. Captain Taskin-Ud-Din went from 'A' to 'C' Company while Captain Mehdi and Captain Bell were posted to 'E' from 'B' and 'C' Companies respectively.

The following officers arrived and were posted to Companies:

Captain P. S. Gill, Indian Signal Corps to 'E' Coy.
Captain Charan Singh, 16th Punjab Regiment to 'D' Coy.
Captain M. A. Zahid, MLI to 'D' Coy.

Captain N. A. K. Bishwas, IAOC to 'A' Coy.
Captain S. P. Malhotra, 15th Punjab Regiment to 'B' Coy.
Captain V. V. Vieyra, Kumaon Regiment to 'C' Coy.
Captain J. S. Nakai, Sikh Regiment to 'B' Coy.
Captain K. M. Shahane, Rajputana Rifles to 'E' Coy.
Captain K. C. Amand, RIA to 'C' Coy.
Captain M. I. Khan, RIASC to 'A' Coy.
Captain M. G. Hazari, Dogra Regiment to 'E' Coy.

On 7 June Auchinleck Battalion paraded for the occasion of the passing out from the Academy of 15 cadets of the Second Course. Brigadier Mohd. Akbar Khan, MBE, Commander, Meerut Sub-Area, inspected the Battalion on parade and took the salute.

We congratulate the following cadets on passing out from the Academy and wish them good luck and success in their careers:

No. 105 – GC – C. A. Quinn
No. 94 – GC – A. S. Apte
No. 19 – GC – Gursharan Singh
No. 70 – GC – B. I. Manzoor
No. 77 – GC – J. S. Narrang
No. 41 – GC – N. K. Saksena
No. 107 – GC – P. Bhattacharya
No. 47 – GC – S. P. Mukerjee
No. 54 – GC – G. Narayanan
No. 98 – GC – K. G. Radha Krishnan.
No. 28 – GC – R. G. L. Badshah
No. 104 – GC – A. D. Mohoni
No. 96 – GC – L. M. Nazareth
No. 26 – GC – Mir Aktar Ali Khan
No. 74 – GC – Fateh Khan

Inevitably at the end of the term a number of changes in the Officer Staff of Auchinleck Battalion have occurred and we say goodbye and good luck to those who are leaving and welcome those who come in their place.

Officers Leaving Auchinleck Battalion

Major A. C. Iyappa MBE, ISC
Major T. R. Johnson, FF Regiment
Captain J. R. A. MacMullen MC, Irish Guards

Captain K. C. Perry MC, Royal Engineers
Captain N. A. K. Biswas, IAOC
Captain K. M. Shahane, Rajputana Rifles
Captain M. G. Canning, Coldstream Guards
Captain Taskin-ud-din, FF Rifles
Officers coming to Auchinleck Battalion
Major M. L. Thapan, Rajput Regiment
Captain G. S. Charak, IAOC
Captain H. S. Kochar, RIA
Captain P. B. Gilani, RIASC

IMA Cricket Tour to the UK – June 1947

THE IMA CRICKET TEAM left Dehra Dun on 17 May and embarked at Bombay on 19 May in HMT *Georgic* for the voyage to the United Kingdom. The voyage itself was uneventful, apart from daily energetic PT designed to ensure that all the party arrived in England thoroughly fit and able to do themselves full justice on the cricket field. Great credit is due to Captain R. H. D. Graveston whose work on the boat in this respect made it certain that every member of the party disembarked in splendid health and ready for the hard and concentrated work that lay ahead.

The team arrived in London from Liverpool in the evening of 6 June and went straight to bed in their hotel after some memorable baggage shifting at Euston Station. It is a characteristic of the IMA cricket team that they are always accompanied by enough luggage to support the operations of an Army Corps, and on this occasion they excelled themselves as tin trunks twice the size of Mohoni were trundled at alternative speeds of dead slow and stop from one end to another of Euston Station. In more serious vein it is important for future and similar occasions to ensure that baggage is curtailed to the minimum – 65 lbs. exclusive of cricket kit should more than suffice for a stay of two months or less.

Practice began immediately – at first (owing to two days rain) indoors at Gover's School in Wandsworth, later by kind permission of the MCC at Lords. The initial form displayed as was to be expected after three weeks absence from the game, added to the changed pace of the turf wickets, was patchy and several players took a little time to settle down. In England correct methods pay dividends, and the chancy stroke that is often run productive on the perfect Indian wickets spells danger.

Sitting, left to right: S.N. Manohar, B.S. Aluwalla, Major A.J. Wilson, MC, A.D. Mohoni, Captain R.H.D. Graveston, P.S. Belvalkar.
Standing: M.V. Mujumdar, A.K. Khanna, N. Kazmi, A.E.J. Watts, K. Rabbani, R.S. Garewal, Azhar Sadiq.

It was not long however before the bowlers pronounced themselves satisfied with the conditions, and it became quickly evident that Mazumdar, Belwalkar and Manohar were all going to be dangerous opponents on the responsive turf. Fielding practice, usually watched by a large gallery of spectators drawn away from whatever county match was in progress at the time, was indulged in daily and both speed and accuracy developed admirably. Watts and Belwalkar in particular had admirers for their safe and reliable catching. Archie Fowler in charge of the Lords Nursery, the developer of Denis Compton, was impressed by the form shown and we prepared for the first match confident that we would give a good account of ourselves. It is perhaps pertinent at this juncture to thank the Committee of the MCC and in particular the assistant Secretary Lt Col R. Aird for their kindness to the IMA. Not content with allowing us to practice for a period of ten days at Lords, we were honoured by an invitation to a lunch party at which Lord Lucan said some very kind and welcoming words to us on behalf of the MCC. This official recognition not only greatly eased our path in many ways, but was indicative of the interest taken at the Headquarters of cricket in the development of the game in India.

Osterley Park – Sunday 15 June – Drawn

THE INDIAN GYMKHANA, who included in their team A. H. Kardar (Oxford University and India) and Raiji (Bombay Presidency), batted first and started poorly against some excellent swing bowling by Mazumdar. Adequate support however was not at first forthcoming and all the other bowlers tried, handicapped by a bitterly cold wind, bowled too short on the soft wicket. A. H. Kardar was principally responsible for the Gymkhana recovery hooking particularly well in his score of 87, before being caught and bowled by Major Wilson. Towards the end of the innings Belwalkar's spinners looked difficult, but Mazumdar who bowled splendidly, was clearly the best of the bowlers. The fielding in spite of the cold was good and some good slip catches were taken.

The batsmen faced by an accurate attack found runs difficult to come by, and both Kardar and Ranji demanded respect on a wicket, which was definitely responsive to spin. In the circumstances both Rabbani (in his highest score for the IMA) and Mohoni batted in a most praiseworthy manner. The remaining batsmen made too little use of their feet and were too easily forced on the defensive to look much like scoring prolifically on soft wickets. But this was unquestionably a promising start in unfavourable conditions against strong opponents.

It Was One Night

'What a host of little incidents, all deep buried in the past problems that had been once urgent, arguments that had been keen, anecdotes that were strange just because one remembered ...'

From *Goodbye Mr Chips*

How well do I remember it! Yes, it was one of those ordinary nights, peaceful and quiet. There was the fine cool air of the approaching winter and the departing summer. We were fatigued as usual after the day's security work. There was nothing in nature or otherwise to suggest that that important night, that moment, that event, the dullness and common-placeness of that day, predicted something which no one understood.

People were sitting as usual and chatting. Their faces were shining – flushed with beer. The smoke of their cigarettes – suggested to the more imaginitive the mills of Lancashire. Everyone was moving in a dream. So at least, it appeared to one who contemplates that day, that hour, that moment.

There we were at the appointed hour to be addressed by our CO. We had no clue to what it was to be. We continued to wait. I felt excited. Perhaps to hide it, I started staring at *The Statesman.* I could sense disaster even through the print. We could feel, as Nehru once said, 'the burning heat of the neighbouring cities'.

The flow of refugees into the camps made one doubt the very essence of goodness in human nature. It took one's mind back to the days of the reign of terror in France, to the days of the Russian Revolution, far back to the realms of the English Civil War, or to the days of ancient Rome when Anthony set afoot the mischiefs of war 'with carrion men groaning for burial'. Religion followed in streams of blood and terror was its theme, with spite, hatred and vengeance following suit.

'Stand up, gentlemen' said our SUO. My trance was broken and I stood up, waiting for our CO to say something.

'Zero hour has come' said our CO. 'The Pakistan cadets have to move off from the Academy, within eight hours ...' His voice grew feebler and feebler. I cannot even recollect what he said.

Human relations are at times stronger than political theories. The hearts that were blended together on the playing fields were to be sundered. The cadets were told that they belonged to two different nations. The warmth that endured amongst friends had to be smothered in political theories. Life had to be endured and not lived. The man in the moon smiled. The moon did not rise for us that day.

The echo of the flowing Tons reached us through the chill air of that quiet night singing the same old song 'Men may come and men may go, but I go on for ever'. Nature was mocking at man. Man at his worst and nature at her best stood at strange contrast. They seemed even to foretell the future, of the destruction of the rapturous beauty of Kashmir, to the bloodshed and murder that was to stain our natural history.

That moment, that night, that day has passed. That moment, that night, that day will never repeat itself on God's Earth. But the echoes of that day, that night, that moment still linger in the corners of our memory. We shall never forget it.

Yes, it was one night, peaceful and quiet. But it was a night we shall remember long.

G. C. N. R. Swamy

Farewell

THE YEAR 1947 was indeed a sad one for the IMA in many ways, for amidst the joy and jubilation of Independence we had to suffer many sad partings from long trusted friends, friends of all communities, friends from East and West, with whom we had formed unbreakable bonds -bonds of comradeship, which are greater than the bonds of political thought, bonds of the heart and soul, which outlive political frontiers and national boundaries.

As expressed in 'It was one night', the sudden realisation of this fact was brought home to us most forcibly. With the departure of the Pakistan Cadets, we lost overnight many well-tried friends, companions in work and strife, in love and joy, in healthy rivalry – both on the field of sport and in the realm of debate. For many days after this parting, 'a sudden stillness filled the air'. A drowsy numbness pained our sense, as though of hemlock we had drunk – as Keats might have said.

This sad parting was soon followed by the Pakistan Officers and all the attached staff, from VCOs to Malis. In each strata of social life a friend was lost. Our greatest loss was undoubtedly in that of Major 'Turk' Rahman, who possessed that rare quality of being able to lead unselfishly, always giving credit to another and thus commanding the respect, love and friendship of all who came in contact with him. He and his wife, Farhat and his brother officers who left us on this sad occasion, will long be cherished in our memories.

The exodus of the British Officers and BORs was soon to follow and to leave us poorer in friendship.

Like most 'exoduses' this was carried out over a period of months and therefore the loss was not so apparent at first, but now on looking back we fully appreciate our heavy losses.

Brigadier A. B. Baltrop OBE, MC, known familiary as 'Groppi' was our Commandant, and the mainstay of the Academy. He saw us through the tremendous task of reorganisation – the change over from OTS with its wartime needs, to Military Academy once more, with its peacetime requirements. This 'miracle' was achieved in spite of numerous obstacles, all of which he overcame, and great tribute is due to him and his Senior Officers, nearly all of whom have now left us, for the smoothness and eficiency with which this task was accomplished.

We bid him and Mrs Baltrop, whose dignified presence was always an inspiration, a sad farewell and wish them our profoundest thanks and ensure them of our lasting respect and loyalty.

Colonel H. R. Power – 'Pom' Power to his friends – and we were all his friends – was our last Deputy Commandant. His association with the IMA dated back many years, and all who knew him and Mrs Power will always remember their unbounding cheerfulness, their deep and sympathetic understanding of all who came in contact with them. Their laughter will long ring in the halls of the IMA.

Lieut-Col E. C. Gould, that profound philosopher and linguist with his charming wife – Ernest and Valgy to us – taught us the true meaning of the Importance of Being Earnest, with an unforgettable sense of humour. To them we extend our best wishes for a succesful career in the future wherever they may be.

In Lt Colonel W. R. Holman MC and his accomplished wife, we lost two great friends, the loss to the Riding Club and the IMA Theatre being irreparable.

To Jim Wilson, our Adjutant we extend our heartiest congratulations in seeing his labours rewarded by the award of the MBE in the New Year Honours List and in his appointment as Private Secretary of Gen. D. D. Gracey, Commander-in-Chief of the Pakistan Army. It was largely due to him also that the IMA cricket team gained such outstanding success.

In Don Washtell we lost perhaps the most popular officer and certainly the most inspiring lecturer – whose quips made lectures a joy to listen to and whose superb acting in *Arms and the Man* will not be forgotten. His wife, whose talents are too numerous to mention in detail, helped to colour the lectures with delightful posters and diagrams, and whose designing and acting enriched and enhanced the reputation of the IMA Dramatic Club. Don will also be long remembered as an all-round sportsman.

We owe a tribute also to 'Doc' Livingston, our patient and cheerful MO, to Pat Stubbs for his inspiration and joie de vivre, to Berty Bevan for his tireless energy as Officer i/e Administration and to Gerry Beale and his charming wife and sister-in-law who, with Jean Harley and her husband David and Peter Gorb entertained us so royally on the stage. David will long be remembered for his reorganising of the IMA Museum.

We will not easily forget our Berties and Johnies, our Logans and Dicks, our Peters and Philips, our Guardsmen and Frontier Forcemen, our Infantrymen and Cavalrymen, our Gunners and Parachutists. Each of you has left an impression, each has added a stone to the edifice which will soon become the National War Academy of India.

In the library we often talk of Mr Jackson who for so many years worked so tirelessly as our Librarian.

Our losses have been sorely felt on the Parade ground, in the Central Office, in the 'Q' stores, in the MT Section and on the PT Staff. RSM McGarrity's voice still echoes on parades, and his dignified bearing will long haunt the Drill Square. The IMA will not forget his magnificent example, the perfect Guardsman on parade, the strictest and yet the most respected and popular disciplinarian. With his name will also be remembered his worthy contemporaries, such names as Stone, Prestige, Beardmore, Jones, Tremain and Wheeler. These and many others will long be cherished and repeated again and again. We will not forget your unselfishness, your tireless energy and know that your example will live in the hearts of every officer who was fotunate enought to be your pupil and your friend.

We thank you all, named and unnamed for your share in helping to make this our proud and most cherished institution an inspiration to the youth of India.

We wish you all a fond farewell and hope that you will remember us by sending us your news from time to time and by subscribing to this our Journal, giving us your views and opinions and your helpful criticism. FAREWELL

Part Two

A Tribute

Major General Thakur Mahadeo Singh, DSO

'OLD SOLDIERS NEVER DIE, they only fade away', as the saying goes. This brings to mind the name of a distinguished soldier, the Sandhurst trained King Commissioned Indian Officer (KCIO) – Brigadier (later Major General) 'Thakur Mahadeo Singh, DSO – who was the first Indian Commandant of the Indian Military Academy, the premier officer producing establishment of the country, set up in Dehra Dun in 1932. The memory of his inspiring command has not faded from the minds of those officers on the staff who served under him, as also the Gentlemen Cadets who passed out from the IMA during his tenure as the Commandant.

It was a most challenging assignment for the new incumbent. It was a most turbulent and an eventful period, marked by unprecedented activity arising out of the policy of the Indianisation which had been started. Major changes and re-organisation had to be effected at all levels. In January 1949, the Indian Military Academy was redesignated as the Armed Forces Academy with the Military Wing replacing the old IMA and the Joint Services Wing at Clement Town which later moved to Khadavasla as the National Defence Academy. The IMA had indeed almost overnight, in the face of severe handicaps and infrastructural and personnel deficiencies assumed an important place in our country's national life and as a host to the VIP visitors including Governor General Rajagopalachari and Prime Minister Nehru.

The new Commandant thus was faced with new and unmeasured responsibility. He rose upto the challenge splendidly. Not in the best of health at the time owing to the after-effects of a serious air accident he was involved in during the war, our Commandant attacked with all

The Commandant,
Brigadier Thakur Mahadeo Singh DSO

the energy and enthusiasm the tasks assigned, forging a dedicated team and inspiring the entire staff by personal example, to give of their best. His appeal was direct and it made instant impression on the young minds, both faculty and cadets.

The commandant and his graceful consort Mrs Mahadeo Singh, had a knack of establishing a rapport with all the staff members and their families. The atmosphere of bonhomie prevailed at all the social gatherings and club functions.

He was a great advocate of high values in Public Life. He believed in HONESTY and obedience of orders and honoured the commitments declared by the Service headquarters. A secularist to the core, a great gentleman, he was very compassionate by nature and a true humanitarian. He had a sense of humour and kept his cool even during crises.

The Indian Military Academy at the time could not have had a more competent and loyal officer during the turbulent phase of 1947–49. He made a great impact by his complete sincerity, devotion and self-discipline. I, for one, as the first Indian Adjutant could not have wished for a more considerate, understanding and efficient superior.

Lt Gen. S. P. Malhotra, PVSM

Lieutenant General S. P. Malhotra

First Indian Adjutant of the IMA

IT WAS OBVIOUS IMMEDIATELY after Independence Day in 1947 that the IMA would need to appoint an Indian Adjutant as soon as the right candidate could be found. It was probable, and desirable in the interests of continuity, that we would not have to look further than the outstanding group of Indian instructors already serving at the Academy. I discussed the matter with Groppi, the retiring British Commandant, and Mahadeo Singh, then still Senior Instructor, but already selected as Commandant designate. I was told to produce a recommendation for them both to consider.

My task did not prove difficult. 'Smoky' Malhotra stood out clearly. A man of presence, impeccable manners and beautifully turned out, he had the highest standards himself and demanded them from others. He was just the right kind of officer to act as a role model for the cadets in general, and the Under Officers in particular. I had no doubt that Malhotra would prove an outstanding Adjutant and was delighted, but not surprised, that he did the job so well.

'Smoky' had a distinguished subsequent career, and we kept in touch periodically as he rose towards the top of the Indian Army. In 1965, when I was Chief of Staff in the UN Force in Cyprus to General Thimayya, a previous Commandant of the IMA, Malhotra was commanding his battalion with distinction in the UNEF – based in the Gaza Strip. Thimayya shared my high regard for Malhotra, and regarded him as a future higher commander. When, sadly, Thimayya died suddenly in December 1965, it was appropriate that the Indian guard

Officers of the IMA after Independence – 1947.

of honour sent to escort his body home should come from Malhotra's battalion. They were beautifully turned out, and their drill, of the IMA quality which Malhotra had demanded.

Later I saw him on my visits to India, and was delighted when he reached three star rank, first as Adjutant General and later in an important field command. He paid me a visit in England, and my family have happy memories of his company on that occasion.

Altogether 'Smoky' Malhotra was a fine soldier, greatly admired and respected. I was fortunate to have served with him and to have been able to see something of him after we both left the IMA. He served the Academy well, and was rightly proud of having been its Adjutant.

James Wilson
(Adjutant, IMA, 1945–47)

Passing-Out Parade, 1947

THE SECOND POST-WAR TRAINING course held at the Indian Military Academy ended on December 20 1947 when 189 Gentlemen Cadets recieved their Regular Commissions.

In the presence of about 1000 Civil and Military Guests – a record attendance, an impressive and dignified Ceremonial parade of Gentlemen Cadets was held when the Honourable Sardar Baldev Singh, Defence Minister, took the salute.

The Parade was formed up along the inspection line under the command of GC Academy Senior Under Officer Harbhajan Singh Grewal. The King's Colours were carried by GC Junior Under Officer Mathur and Regimental Colours by GC Junior Under Officer Dharmani.

The Honourable Defence Minister accompanied by Brigadier Thakur Mahadeo Singh DSO, the Commandant and his staff arrived punctually at 0930 and took up his position at the Saluting Base. The Honourable Minister was given a 'General Salute' with all spectators standing.

Led by Gentlemen Cadets Whig and Bannerjee, who were in attendance as Orderlies, the Honourable Defence Minister inspected the Parade. Following the inspection Sardar Baldev Singh addressed the Cadets briefly on the importance of their Career in the Army. After the address the Honourable Defence Minister performed the 'National Flag Hosting Ceremony'. He then decorated Lt Colonel Zorawar Singh, Central India Horse, with the ribbon of the Military Cross, and Sub-Major Hoshiar Singh Gurung with the ribbbon of the Order of British India, Second Class. The Honourable Minister than presented Gold and Silver medals for the cadets passing out First and Second to GC Academy Senior Under Officer Harbhajan Singh Grewal and GC

Left to right:

Sitting: JUO S.S. Gill, Cadet Adjt R.M. Reddy, SUO R.S. Pathania, SUO Indar Singh, Academy SUO H.B.S. Grewal, SUO Z.K. Wadia, SUO S.N. Gurung, SUO Jai Krishna, JUO H.S. Sodhi

2nd row standing: JUO K. Chiman Singh, JUO G.B. Phillips, C.Q.M.S. K.S. Grewal, CSM S.N. Verma, JUO H.C. Dutta, JUO S.K. Mathur, JUO T.C. Dharmani, JUO G.A. Nagle, JUO M.L. Chibber, CSM K.B. Pillay, CSM B.S. Grewal, JUO G.S. Rawat, JUO D. Katoch

3rd row standing: CQMS J.S. Khurana, CQMS M. Rawlins, JUO A.C. Katoch, JUO T.N. Luther, JUO K. Bannerjee, CSM J.S. Negi, CQMS K. Balaram, CQMS J.R. Rebello, CSM B. Chatterjee, JUO N.G.K. Nair, JUO A.S. Cheema, JUO B. Lall, JUO M.L. Chadha

---

Senior Under Officer Jai Krishna. Finally the Governor General's Banner was presented to Cassino Coy – the champion Company for the year 1947.

The passing out Cadets then marched past.

For ordinary spectators perhaps the first impressions, which were the most inspiring, were the March on to the parade ground by the Cadets. The Band also presented a very bright picture.

The Cadets that morning never failed nor faltered for a moment. Their steadiness when halted and the prescision of their movements were impeccable.

The supreme competence and confidence with which the Gentlemen Cadets bore their part in the Ceremony under their own Cadet Under Officers and NCOs were most noteworthy.

They have good reason to be proud of their achievements.

S. P. Malhotra

Editorial – June 1948

ONCE MORE A VERY EVENTFUL TERM has passed. No sooner had the term begun that the tragic news of the Mahatma's death was announced to the world. The IMA Tennis Team was on its way to Delhi and had heard the news at Meerut. In Delhi, needless to say no matches were played and no offices or shops were open, but one and all, rich and poor, flocked to Kingsway and other vantage points to catch a last glimpse of the great man. Never has Delhi seen such an orderly crowd. Murmurs arose as the funeral bier, around which sat the Governor General, The Prime Minister, The Deputy Prime Minister, The Defence Minister and the Mahatma's granddaughters passed slowly and majesticaly towards Rajghat.

Mahatma Gandhi
2 October 1869 – 30 January 1948.

After 14 days of mourning, normal life was resumed, and on 13 February The Governor General accompanied by Lady Mountbatten honoured the Academy with a visit which was short, but left an everlasting impression on the minds of both officers and cadets. The Governor General inspected Field Training, Drill and Instructional periods and other activities at the

Above: Commandant and Officers

Left: His Excellency, The Governor General of India, Lord Louis Mountbatten of Burma KG, GCVO, KCB, DSO

Academy. Before leaving Lord Mountbatten gave a most inspiring address to offices and cadets in historic Chetwode Hall. Extracts of his address are published on another page, so more need not be said here, except that this great sailor and statesman left a part of himself behind and there was not a man who did not leave that hall a wiser and better man, so great was the personality of the speaker. Here was an example of a born leader.

Their Excellencies' visit was especially notable for its friendliness and informality. The combination of a proved great leader of armed forces in the field and a Governor General is very rare, and so this visit was a unique occasion for the Academy.

The next important official visit was that of the Adjutant General in India, Major Gen. S. M. Shrinagesh, the first Indian Officer to hold this appointment. Gen. Shrinagesh's visit was less formal and lasted 3 days, from 23 to 25 April, which gave him time to see the Academy from many angles. His address was most enlightening and inspired cadets and officers alike. He was no new visitor, having been the first Indian Coy. Comd. here in 1940.

On Friday and Saturday 28 and 29 May the Commander-in-Chief, General F. R. R. Bucher CB, OBE, MC, visited the Academy accompanied by the Quartermaster General in India, Maj. General S. B. S. Chimni OBE and the Director of Military Training Brigadier (now Maj. General) J. H. Wilkinson CIE.

The Commander-in-Chief's programme included an inspection of the Close Quarter Battle Range, a visit to the IMA Cinema where a man Management film *Officer and Man* was being screened, an inspection of the IMA Museum, Library and Methods Factory, and an inspection of the instructional classes.

In the afternoon the DMT gave a talk on Discipline to officers and cadets.

On the 28 evening the Commander-in-Chief dined in the Cadet's Mess and attended a Musical Concert given by cadets.

On the morning of Saturday 29 May, General Bucher took the salute at the End of Term Parade.

On this occasion the following cadets recieved their Commissions:

GC	K. R. S. Bhinder
GC	K. C. Aiyanna
GC	R. R. J. Snaize
GC	P. S. Bhelvalkar
GC	K. Goswami
GC	S. P. R. Salunke
GC	N. L. Iyengar
GC	R. Mitra
GC	J. Nayar
GC	B. R. Mulay

We congratulate them all.

Top: The Governor General inspecting Cadets on Parade

Middle: Lord Mountbatten, Brigadier Mahadeo Singh and Colonel Misra

Bottom: Lord and Lady Mountbatten with Mrs. Mahadeo Singh watching field training

The Prime Minister's Visit

8 December 1948

THE HONOURABLE PANDIT JAWAHARLAL NEHRU, the Honourable Sardar Baldev Singh and party arrived at Sarsava airfield on the afternoon of 8 December 1948 and were met by the Commandant, Brigadier Mahadeo Singh DSO and the GI, Lt Col P. S. Bhagat VC, who accompanied them to the Commandant's House.

In the evening the Prime Minister and Defence Minister, dined in Mess, where the Prime Minister was introduced to the Officers of the IMA and Officers of the Interservices Wing.

Among the guests were HH the Maharajah of Patiala, Air-Marshal Sir Thomas Elmhirst, Vice-Admiral W. E. Parry, Mr A. V. Pai, Lt Gen. Russell and Maj. Gen. Kalwant Singh. We were glad to see once more Col L. T. Firbank, Lt Col M. L. Thapan and Maj. Y. R. Puri, all former IMA Officers.

After dinner the Prime Minister presented trophies to the companies. In the meantime, the wives of distinguished visitors, including Lady Elmhirst, Mrs Parry, Mrs Russell and Mrs Kalwant Singh, were entertained to dinner in the Café by Mrs Mahadeo Singh and the officers' wives.

At 9.30 p. m. the Prime Minister was escorted to the IMA Theatre, where he was entertained by the Music Circle and Dramatic Club at their end of term concert, Passing Show II, which in addition to musical items, including a performance of *The Scheming Lieutenant* by Sheridan. After the show Pandit Nehru presented bouquets to Mrs Wright, Mrs Russell and Miss Chatterji.

On the morning of 9 December, the Prime Minister took the Salute at the Passing-Out Parade of the First Ex-University Graduates Course, and presented SUO Ved Prakash with a Silver Medal, as the best cadet. The Parade was commanded by Academy SUO Himmeth Singh.

Never has such a large gathering been seen on the Parade ground. Numerous refugees from the Refugees Camp, wishing to catch a glimpse of 'Panditji', invaded the Drill Square, and many had to be turned away.

In his address the Prime Minister reminded Cadets that the Indian Army had a great tradition and pointed out that on their good behaviour rested 'the fair name and future greatness of the Army'.

Editor's Notes

December 1948

THE YEAR WHICH DRAWS TO A CLOSE as we go to press with this edition of the *Indian Military Academy Journal* is the momentous year of Independence, the year of liberation of a fifth of the human race from political bondage. With Independence came partition with its brood of ills and woes. We have good reason to be proud of the part played by the Academy during the disturbances in maintaining law and order.

With these political changes also came partings. We miss many familiar faces and welcome warmly all the new additions to the IMA family. We join our Commandant, Brigadier Thakur Mahadeo Singh DSO, in wishing all success to those officers who left us for Pakistan to form the nucleus of the Pakistan Military Academy.

Life at the Academy goes on as smoothly as ever. In these eventful and troublesome times the IMA seems a haven of order, peace and tranquility. The only difference is that instead of the Union Jack the glorious Tricolour flutters proudly over Chetwode Building.

We congratulate Cassino Company on winning both the King George V and Governor General's Banners. The results of the competitions are as follows:

	King George V Banner		*Governor General's Banner*	
1.	Cassino Company	22 points	Casssino Company	12 points
2.	Sangro Company	21 points	Imphal Company	9 points
3.	Imphal Company	17 points	Sangro Company	5 points
4.	Meiktila Company	16 points	Alamein Company	5 points
5.	Alamein Company	4 points	Meiktila Company	2 points

The Passing Out Parade this year was the most memorable event in the history of the IMA. Never before was such a throng of enthusiastic visitors welcomed at the Academy. The Honourable Defence Minister Sardar Baldev Singh hoisted the National Flag to the moving strains of Jana Gana Mana and we doubt if there was any heart in the whole assembly which did not throb with pride, joy and thankfulness when 189 cadets slow marched into the portals of Chetwode Hall as the band played *Auld Lang Syne.* Extracts from Extempore Address by his Excellency Rear Admiral the Earl Mountbatten of Burma to the Indian Military Academy on 13 February 1948.

Editorial

December 1948

THIS PERHAPS HAS BEEN the most eventful term the IMA has experienced in recent years.

The 3rd Course Cadets returned at the end of July to hear that they were to be commissioned in September, consequently the first six weeks of term were spent in unprecedented activity.

At the end of July her Excellencey, Mrs Sarojini Naidu, Governor of the UP, honoured the Academy with a visit. Her stay though very brief, was indeed memorable and coincided with the return of the 1st Ex-University Graduates Course. The informality of Her Excellency's visit is well expressed in the photographs published on another page.

Independence Day was celebrated on 15 August – the first anniversary of a truly historic event, a short article on which is published with this issue.

This event was followed by a visit from Lt Gen. Thakur Nathu Singh, GOC Eastern Command and a two day session of the National War Academy Syllabus Committee, under the able chairmanship of Dr Amarnath Jha.

On 11 September the great day for the 3rd Course arrived. The Honourable Sardar Baldev Singh, Defence Minister took the salute at the passing-out parade, when 185 Gentlemen Cadets marched off the square for the last time. An article on this great event entitled 'A visit to the IMA' by Brigadier S. C. Misra will be found on another page. The day was concluded with a successful concert entitled 'Passing Show' organised by Maj. Mukand.

Barely a month was to pass before His Excellency the Governor-General Shri Rajagopalachari, honoured the Academy with his presence.

Unfortunately the weather did not benefit the occasion, rain somewhat marring the outdoor activities. His Excellency's visit is reported on in another article with illustrations.

On Saturday 25 September the Kashmir Ball in aid of the troops fighting in Kashmir was held at the Dehra Dun Club, and the handsome sum of over Rs. 2,000 was collected from the proceeds. The IMA was particularly proud of the Sweet Stall set up and decorated by the IMA Officers' Wives.

Undaunted the IMA Ladies then started out on a knitting campaign during which 20 lbs of khaki wool was converted into scarves, balaclava caps, mittens, gloves, socks and pullovers for the troops in Kashmir. This was so successful that Lady Bucher sent a further consignment of wool, which is being attacked in earnest.

October and November will be remembered largely for the number of camps held, most notable of which was Exercise Chindit which is reported on fully elsewhere.

Then came assessment and interviews and banner marches, all in the short period of a few weeks, to be crowned by the Prime Minister's Visit on the 8 and 9 December and Inauguration Day celebrations on 10 December. Everyone, Staff and Cadets are now earning a well deserved rest of 4 weeks, an extra week having been added to the Winter Vacation.

In January, we reopen as the Armed Forces Academy with two wings, the Military Wing replacing the old IMA and the Interservice Wing at Clement Town. Here Cadets between the ages of 15 and 17 will be trained for the Army, Navy and Air Force, and already a number of the Staff have arrived.

We congratulate Lt Col Kamta Prasad on being appointed Deputy Commandant of the Interservice Wing and Mr Jack Gibson from the Doon School, on being appointed Principal. In our next number we will publish a special article on the opening of the Interservice Wing.

In conclusion we welcome all those who have joined us recently and bid farewell to many departing friends and wish them all a happy and prosperous New Year.

Special Order of the Day

By Brigadier Thakur Mahadeo Singh DSO
Commandant Indian Military Academy

Dehra Dun, 31 December 1948

THE COMMANDANT HAS GREAT PLEASURE in announcing that the Indian Military Academy will be re-designated as the Armed Forces Academy with effect from 1 January, 1949.

The new Academy will consist of two wings, viz. a Military Wing and an Interservice Wing.

The IMA has every reason to be proud of its past achievements and 1 January, 1949 will be a great day in its history, as an important change is taking place in the training doctrine of the officers of the Armed Forces.

The Armed Forces Academy will be the interim National War Academy, which will thus evolve physically from the present IMA.

The proud and strong traditions and spirit of the IMA have enabled the Interservice training to be started here much earlier than was originally expected.

Our country is the first in the world to start the basis of true Interservices training and co-operation. It is a unique honour and privilege to all members of the Staff and Cadets who will be associated with the initiation of this great experiment.

The Commandant is confident that all members will do their utmost to make the AFA the success it deserves to be.

Though separated by distance the Commandant wishes to impress that both wings are integral parts of the Academy and every effort should be made to bring out the true Interservice co-operation and comradeship. Each wing should study the functions of the other, and all members by mutual trust, respect and understanding should foster and cement complete loyalty and unity to the Armed Forces Academy.

The IMA has done it and the AFA will also do it.

The Commandant takes this opportunity to wish every one all success in the coming year especially as, in this year, the true foundation of the NWA will be laid with the whole object of Service to our Country and the Armed Forces.

Arrivals

AMONG the new arrivals since our last number was published we welcome among others:

Col Harbakhsh Singh, our new and very popular Deputy Commandant.

Lt Col P. S. Bhagat VC, our cheerful and efficient G–1.

Lt Col Budh Singh MC, our ever smiling Senior Instructor.

Lt Col Shiv Dayal Singh, Commander of Meiktila Company, the Champion Company this year.

Major R. L. Mullick, our new Sub-Editor and IAEC Instructor.

Major H. R. H. Daniell, the never tiring officer I/C English and the ever popular Dramatic Club.

We also are glad to welcome back British Warrant Officers and Sergeants, 20 of whom have arrived to take up duties in both the Military and Interservice Wings. In particular we welcome the return of 3 former Instructors RSMs Prestige, Morris, Hill.

Departures

BEFORE HALF TERM we lost Maj. S. J. Mukand, a very popular and enthusiastic officer. Not only will we miss him in the lecture hall, but also from the ranks of the Music Circle, Literary and Debating Society and the Dramatic Club, for which clubs he did so much. With him we also lose his beautiful partner and accomplished actress, Lalita, always to be remembered in her role as Arjuna in *Chitra*, which part she played with dignity and grace. In bidding both of them farewell we congratulate them on their promotion to Lt Col and Commandant of the Army School of Education, Pachmarhi, and Lady-in-Charge of Welfare Pachmarhi respectively. Our loss is Pachmarhi's gain.

We also bid farewell to Capt. Bhargava, who will be sorely missed at the Bridge table and as a Hockey Referee, and Capt. V. D. Shrike, who left us to rejoin Baroda State Forces.

Extracts from Earl Mountbatten's Address

Extempore Address by his Excellency Rear Admiral the Earl Mountbatten of Burma to the Indian Military Academy on 13 February 1948

IT IS A VERY GREAT THRILL to me to have a chance to come up and visit the Indian Military Academy, particularly at this time, because the Indian Military Academy is training the future officers of the Army, the Army of a free India, at a moment which is probably the most important in Indian History. Now the Army is of course essential in war. But people are apt to think that in peacetime is only there being got ready for war. That is not so in any country, but particularly not in the case of India, because in the case of India it is the presence of the Army of well-disciplined, entirely impartial loyal men, that causes stability at times of trouble such as we have been passing through.

It is for the Army, more than any other organised unit in the country, both to set an example and to bring about the policy for which Mahatma Gandhi gave his life, that is, of a unified India without any communal bitterness or ill feeling. It is for the Army to carry out the policy of the Government which Pandit Nehru has laid down, which is to build a great secular state in India in which everybody is going to have opportunities the like of which have never been seen before in India. And to do that I don't need to tell you that you must never in any circumstances mix politics with soldiering. That doesn't mean to say everybody should not have their own views

The Hon. Defence Minister, the Hon. Prime Minister and the Commandant standing before the Governor General's Photograph in the Officers' Mess.

on politics, but it does mean to say that your first loyalty is to the Government and to the Service. Your personal feelings must be subordinate to that.

Now, throughout the world in all the Armed Forces, scientific development is moving at so rapid a pace that mechanisation and scientific development are the order of the day in practically every Army. It is necessary, therefore, to have officers and technical men who have special education and training to enable them to work these various mechanical gadgets. But will you please remember that machines don't run themselves. Every machine has to be run by a man and ultimately the whole thing depends on the man and his working the machine. And so pay the greatest possible attention to the man. I am sure you have often been told that, but I wonder if you realise that it is not just a platitude.

Now here you have a great opportunity of acquiring not only education, but of developing your character in such a way that it will fit you to be among the world's finest officers. Education is not a thing that can be spoon-fed into you like medicine. You have to pick it up for yourselves. Often one doesn't appreciate the immense value of the opportunity of being at a college while one is still there.

It is important also to make up your mind what sort of a character it is that you want to develop. Many people have tried to define it, but it is not easy to put into words. I suggest that you want to be the sort of man that other men look up to. I don't mean only your subordinates or your contemporaries, but also your senior officers. How can you become that? First of all I think by setting yourselves a standard of integrity, of moral and intellectual honesty so that you yourselves never deceive yourselves, but know exactly where you stand. Develop wide open minds so that you can see both sides of any subject and other persons' points of view. Strive for a reputation of fairmindedness which is justified because you really are fairminded, so that when you come to make a decision, people will have confidence in it and know it is honest. After that you must have the moral courage to stand by that decision, even at a time when it might prove to be unpopular and cause you to be jeered at.

To acquire this in your character you have got to work hard. It will not just come to you by itself. You have got to make the most of your opportunities here. Think to yourselves every day – am I improving? It is no good sitting back and saying when you leave here – 'I have been to the Indian Military Academy, I am an old gentleman cadet, therefore I am a good officer' because believe me although you ought to be a good officer, many men who have risen from the ranks or entered without the facilities you have here, will be better officers than you if you have not made the most of your opportunities.

What is courage? It is not just being unafraid, for no one can help it if he feels afraid, but the quality an officer requires is, I suggest, not showing his emotions. Twice I slipped up on that and if it helps you to understand what I mean I don't mind confessing it.

I remember in my first night action of this war, after my flotilla leader the 'Kelly' had been torpedoed off a German minefield in the North Sea, an enemy E-boat came out of the darkness and opened fire as it shot past us at the bridge on which I was standing with a 20 mm pom pom. This was at 2030 yards range. I was alone on the bridge as my damaged ship was being towed back and the survivors were busy trying to prevent the ship from turning over. I ducked down behind the bridge screen a very silly thing to do, for it would not have kept out a rifle bullet. Then I suddenly felt frightfully ashamed and very glad I was alone on the bridge so that no one had seen me duck. I said to myself 'Never again will I permit myself to show when I am afraid'.

It is unpleasant being bombed at sea, but far more unpleasant in harbour where one is a sitting target. In order that the men's nerves should not be unduly strained by those endless attacks I ordered half the ship's company of each ship should go into the rock shelters in Malta harbour. I said that either the Captain or the second-in-command was to be on board and that the other should be in the shelter. I gave the order, but I had not the moral courage to obey my own orders. There was nobody to give me the order and so I stayed on board. I hated it every time we were attacked, frightened of what my friends would say if my ship were sunk while I was in a shelter.

My time is running out and I want to end up by reminding you that the fighting services of the country can no longer remain in watertight compartments. I had the privilege in the last war of being chosen to start off the Combined Operation Headquarters which was the first interservice inter-allied headquarters I think, in history. I then had the inspiring experience of having to get up a similar interservice inter-allied Headquarters in South East Asia. then I learnt that the three services have got to work as one. Officers have got to know those of the other services and work together.

I threw what weight I could into the scale in this direction, when the question of how young Indian Officers were to be trained for war was brought up by Field Marshal Auchinleck, I was as keen as he was that there should be a National War Academy in which the three Services would have their young officers trained together. This is to be built eventually at Karakawasla near Poona and building sites have been earmarked, but it will take at least seven years to put up all the buildings. I am glad to be able to tell you that there are proposals now under examination in the Ministry of Defence to start something on the same lines right here at Dehra Dun in the first instance. It has not yet been officially approved, but I hope that it will be in the near future. I cannot imagine more perfect surroundings in which to start such a vital scheme off.

You are going to be officers of a great historical moment in the history of India. The Army can do more than any other Service for India to make her great, but you must work in well with the other two services. I wish you all the very best of luck.

The National War Academy

By Brigadier S. P. P. Thorat, DSO

THE INDIAN ARMY won undying fame for its gallantry and devotion to duty in World War I. World War II gave an opportunity to the Royal Indian Navy and the Royal Indian Air Force to prove their worth – which they did in no uncertain manner. Today the Defence Forces of India perhaps the only voluntary army of sailors, soldiers and airmen which braved the last mighty war – are a proven force equal to the best in the world. This magnificent Force has contributed substantially to India's progress towards freedom and has enabled her to stand in line with the other great nations of the world on an equal plane. Now that India is where she is on the political map of the world, she needs must have everything of the best to facilitate her future progress towards being a worthy member of the world order. This is the basis on which the National War Academy is being planned.

The idea of setting up a national academy was first mooted in the year 1941 when the Sudan Government paid a glowing tribute to the gallantry of Indian troops by placing the huge sum of £100,000 at the disposal of the then Viceroy, Lord Linlithgow. The gift, it was suggested should be utilised for erecting a suitable war memorial and many thought then that this war memorial should take the shape of an institution for imparting military education. This idea, however, did not come to the forefront until Field Marshall Sir Claude Auchinleck returned to India in 1943 to take up the appointment of Commander-in-Chief for the second time. Already a great admirer of India and her fighting men, Sir Claude had now returned with fresh memories of the Indian Army's brilliant achievements on the field and consequently he took up the question of a national war memorial with great zeal. Many ideas regarding the war memorial had already been put forward including Prof. Hill's suggestion of a Centre for Medical Education and Research. The Commander-in-Chief, while recognising the educational and medical needs of the country, was however, of the opinion that a National War Memorial should be closely linked with the Fighting Services and be of direct interest and benefit to them. He therefore put forward his own suggestion of an interservices academy. Elaborating the scheme he wrote to the Viceroy on 25 August 1944 'India is likely, sooner or later, to attain her full status as a nation as a result of the part she has played in the War. It would be fitting that this part should be commemorated by a memorial which will not only help to provide her with leaders for the Fighting Forces, whose task it will be to preserve her national status in the future, but it will also provide a model for educational institutions throughout the country'.

The Commander-in-Chief's suggestion was readily accepted by the Government and a committee was appointed on 2 May 1945 to prepare a scheme for the establishment of the proposed academy. This committee consisted of the best available talent in the field of education and Service training. It started its work by issuing a comprehensive questionnaire to the public and to certain officers of the Services. A sub-committee was also appointed to study the military, naval and air force training institutions of other nations such as the USA, Canada and the United Kingdom. This sub-committee visited the United States Military Academy at West Point and the Naval Academy at Annapolis, the Royal Military College at Kingston in Canada and the Service academies of Great Britain.

By the time the sub-committee returned to India, the replies to the questionnaire had been received and collated and it had a fair knowledge of public opinion as well as the views of experts. This was a good basis on which to start actual planning. Consequently while the main committee went ahead with general work, two more sub-committees were set up, one to draw up the Syllabus and Establishment and the other to advise on the accommodation and equipment for the proposed academy. The Syllabus sub-committee was composed of eminent educationists and senior members of the Services under the chairmanship of Dr Amarnatha Jha, Vice-Chancellor of Allahabad University. The programme of academic instruction recommended by them has now been accepted by the Inter-University Board of India as comparing favourably with the Degree standard of Indian Universities. The

Accommodation sub-committee had at its head Brigadier D. R. Bateman then Director of Military Training.

After carefully considering the recommendations of the various sub-committees, the Working Commmittee framed its final report which is under examination by the Government at present. The report which is a comprehensive document, describes in detail the constitution proposed for the National War Academy. Its main features are as under:

1. The Academy should be known as the National War Academy and should train officers for the RIN the Army and the RIAF
2. Candidates wishing to join the Academy should have passed their 16th birthday but not reached their 19th birthday and should have passed the Matriculation or an equivalent examination.
3. The only criterion for selection to the Academy should be merit and that no vacancies should be reserved either for provinces, communities or even for sons of servicemen.
4. All cadets should be required to undertake to serve as regular officers (or in certain cases as officers in the Reserve after serving for a short period with 'the colours') on passing out.
5. That the course at the Academy should be of four years duration and that tuition, messing and clothing at the Academy should be free.
6. The Academy should be the main though not the only channel of entry into the Services.
7. The aim of the Academy should be to train and instruct cadets so that on satisfactory completion of the course, each cadet will have the requisite educational and professional standard and shall have acquired the mental, moral and physical qualities essential to his progressive and continued development as an officer of the Defence Forces of India.

The training at the Academy will be spread over a period of four years, each year consisting of approximately 44 working weeks. The programme for 36 weeks which will comprise the Academic year, will consist of 1,188 periods for academic instruction, 432 periods for service training and 72 periods for ceremonial drill, duration of each period being 50 minutes. The remaining eight weeks will be spent in training camps. During the first two years all cadets will pursue a common course of study. In the third and fourth year specialised instruction in various subjects will be given bearing in mind the needs of the particular service to which the cadet is to be assigned. All cadets will do short attachments to all the three Services.

The proposed annual intake of 600 cadets is based on the provisional data supplied by the Defence Department. The intake must however conform with the officer requirements of the Defence Forces and is therefore liable to alteration. The present planning is however based on a provisional intake of 600 cadets annuallly and it is estimated that round the magnificent buildings of the Academy will spring up a self-sufficient town of nearly 16,000 inhabitants connected with the Academy in one way or the other.

The proposed site for the Academy is ideal for an all-weather habitation. Away from the din and noise of busy humanity, the Karakwasla area, interspersed with small picturesque hills, is about eleven miles from Poona. Hedged in by the deep clear waters of the lake on one side and by a ring of hills on the other three, it is one of the most pleasing parts of the Deccan. Its altitude (2,000 to 3,000 feet) its freedom from alluvial deposits and the prevalence of Westerly breezes make its dry, invigorating air well suited to people from all parts of the country. Here the heat is less oppressive and the cold more comfortable than in most parts of India. Population around this area is very thin and hence its acquisition will cause little hardship to local people. The thinly populated area will provide excellent grounds for training in the arts of modern warfare and the lake with its sufficiently deep waters will be suitable for naval training. An airfield will also be located in the vicinity for air training.

It is but natural that many should feel sad at the thought that the Indian Military Academy, the premier Service training institution of India which has built up such enviable traditions of efficiency, selfless service and devotion to duty – which has given thousands of capable officers to the Indian Army and which during its comparatively short existence has proved itself to be one of the finest military academies in the world, will close down when the National War Academy starts working. The IMA however will not 'close down' – it will merely change its name and location and together with certain other Service training institutions, merge itself into the NWA and emerge again in the new shape designed to serve India even better. The NWA will inherit the IMA's proud record and rich traditions and will, for ever, strive to live up to and enhance the fair name of its illustrious Alma Mater – the Indian Military Academy.

NOTE: The reader may be confused by the various names the Academy has had. The original IMA did not become the National War Academy, but the Armed Forces Academy and then the National Defence Academy. When the NDA moved to Karakwasla only the naval and airforce cadets were trained there, the army cadets continued at Dehra Dun and the Academy was renamed the Indian Military Academy.

Inauguration of the Armed Forces Academy

FOURTH JUNE 1949 will ever be remembered as Inauguration Day of the Armed Forces Academy and will commemorate the formation of the first institution in the World to train officers for the three services (Navy, Army and Air Force). As such the Armed Forces Academy is

Inauguration Day Parade: The Quarter Deck.

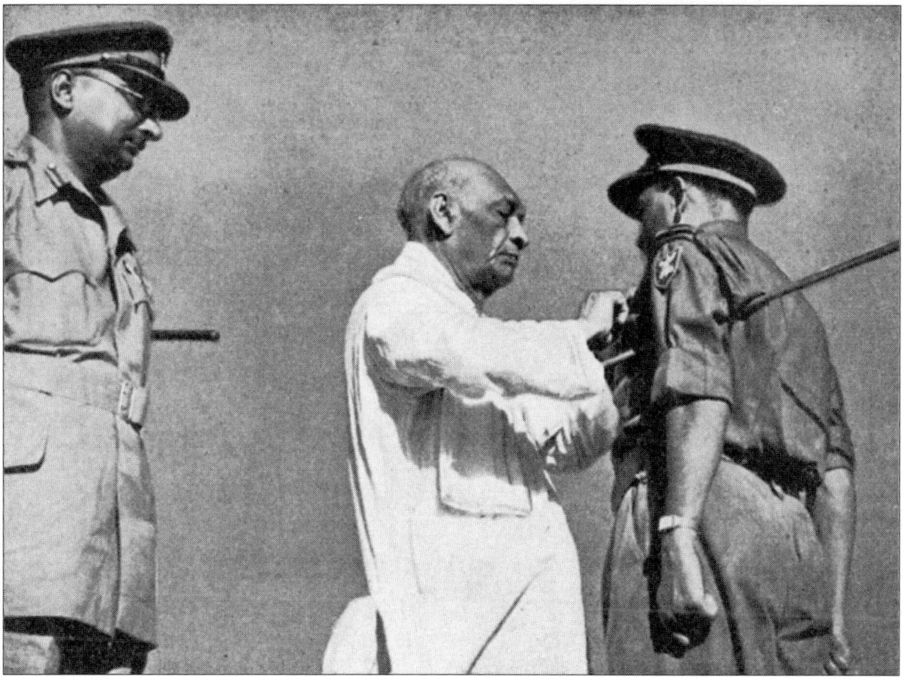

The Deputy Prime Minster presenting Col Kamta Prasad with the Military Cross.

setting an example for all progressive countries to follow. India is proud of being the first country to bring into existence such an institution.

The Armed Forces Academy owes its existence largely to the Indian Military Academy which it has absorbed and expanded, the original IMA becoming the Military Wing. The Interservice Wing, as its name implies, trains cadets (between the ages of 15 to 17) to become Naval, Army and Air Force Officers, that is, it gives these young cadets a basic training, mental, cultural and physical which will enable them to proceed to Naval, Military and Air Forces training centres, according to their aptitude. Thus after 2 years training at the ISW cadets will pass on to more advanced training before being Commissioned into one of the three Services.

Inauguration Day itself was blessed with sunshine in more senses than one, for on this occasion the greatness of India was represented in the person of Shri Vallabhai Patel, the Deputy Prime Minister, Sardar Baldev Singh, Hon'ble Defence Minister, the three Service Chiefs, General K. M. Cariappa, Air Marshall Sir Thomas Elmhirst, and Commodore Drew representing the Naval C-in-C, and many other notables including Lt Gen. G. G. Simmonds of the Royal Canadian Army.

In his address, the Deputy Prime Minister said 'Yours is a truly national institution in which must grow that healthy secular outlook which is the foundation of true democracy and unshakable loyalty to the principles on which that democracy must rest.'

After an impressive parade in which the new ISW cadets played a very creditable role, the Deputy Prime Minister and the numerous guests who witnessed the parade were entertained to breakfast at the Interservice Wing Officers Mess'.

Before the guests dispersed a photograph was taken of the Deputy Prime Minister, Senior guests and Staff of the Armed Forces Academy.

Thus was inaugurated a great national institution, which in the course of years will be absorbed and renamed the National War Academy.

Author with President Rajagopalachari.

Author with Pandit Nehru.

The Military Wing Armed Forces Academy

THE MILITARY WING, formerly the Indian Military Academy, was renamed on the formation of the Armed Forces Academy in January 1949, when the Interservice Wing for Army, Navy and Air Force Cadets, was inaugurated.

From January 1951 the Military Wing will be fed entirely from the Interservice Wing, and will give Army Cadets a further training of two years in addition to the 2 years ISW Training. Thus Army cadets will receive four years training in all, and will be commissioned between the ages of 19 and 20. This increased period of training should greatly benefit Army Cadets and should improve the general standard of entries into the Army.

It may be of interest to readers of Suryodaya to know the past history of the old IMA of the Alma Mater of the Indian Army.

Its History

INAUGURATED IN 1932 by Field Marshall Sir Philip Chetwode then Commander-in-Chief of the Indian Army, the IMA became the Sandhurst of India opening its gates to a select body of men between the ages of 17 ½ and 19 ½. These were chosen as a result of a competitive examination and an interview. 15 cadets were taken from the leading schools of India (the RIMC and the Doon School being prominent among these schools), 15 were selected from the ranks of the Army, open to those holding a Lance Naik's appointment (or above) provided they had passed the First Class Indian Army Certificate of Education.

A further 10 were selected from the States Forces. Thus 40 cadets were selected bi-annually.

The courses were of 2 ½ years duration and the estimated cost of the course was over Rs. 10,000/– of which the cadet's parent paid one third and the Government of India the remaining two thirds.

Now the whole cost of the course is borne by Government.

It was on the first Inauguration Day 10 December 1932 that Sir Philip Chetwode uttered those famous words, which are now engraved in gold lettering on the fine pannelled dais of Chetwode Hall. It is upon these words that the traditions of the Academy are founded.

The six-monthly intake of 40 cadets continued until a complement of 200 cadets was reached. It is interesting to note that the Academy was then officered by 12 officers and one VCO. The Military Wing is now officered by over 60 officers, 9 BORs and some 20 JCOs with a complement of over 700 cadets.

The King Emperor's Cadetship

IN FEBRUARY 1933 the first award of the King Emperor's Cadetship was granted to Kanyha Lal Atal and carried with it a remission of fees to the extent of Rs. 2,120/–. Today the training is free.

The Colours

ON 10 APRIL 1933 the first old colours – the Colours of the 1/11 Sikh Regiment – were committed to the charge of the IMA. These colours to this day hang in place of honour in Chetwode Hall.

The IMA Colours

THE IMA COLOURS – Red and Grey – represent honour and strength in the likeness of blood and steel.

The Buildings

THE ORIGINAL BUILDINGS were built for the Railway Staff Training College, but owing to the World Slump in 1931, the RSTC project had to be abandoned and the buildings and site were taken over by the Government for the establishment of the Indian Military Academy.

Since then many additions have been made, including the Hospital, the Swimming Pool, the Library, the Armoury and additional cadets messes.

In 1936 a cyclone hit the Academy and the roof of the Swimming Pool was badly damaged as well as many buildings belonging to the Contractor.

In 1939 the IMA became an OTS training both British and Indian officers. This continued until 1946 when the IMA returned to its former role and the first post-war course was started.

1947 saw great changes – the departure of the majority of British officers – Partition involving the transfer of all Mohammedan officers and cadets to Pakistan – and the appointment of the first Indian Commandant Brigadier Thakur Mahadeo Singh, DSO, to whom has fallen not only the task of reorganising the IMA, but the formation of the Armed Forces Academy with two wings, the Interservice Wing at Clement Town and the Military Wing at Prem-Nagar.

The strength of the Academy is now over 1,000 students and will increase to a total of 1,600 cadets when the full complement of both wings is reached.

The Honours Boards

THE MILITARY WING can boast of a formidable list of Honours including one VC (2/Lt (now Colonel) P. S. Bhagat, until recently GI at the Military Wing), one George Cross, the George Medal, 3 DSOs, 15 MBEs (including Capt. (now Brigadier) Iyappa of the Indian Signals) 58 HCs, 4HCs of whom are now on the staff of the Military Wing.

Recent Improvements

THIS YEAR SEVERAL ADDITIONS have been made. There are now six companies, Meiktila, the champion company, Imphal, Cassino, Sangro, Kohima and Naushahra, the newest company, all doing a two-year course. In addition, there is Alamein Company, consisting of technical graduates, who are doing a one year's course and who will be commissioned in the RIEs, IEMEs and Signals.

The East Wing

THE OLD BRITISH WING has been renamed East Wing and houses 3 companies (Cassino, Alamein and Naushahra). Six new class rooms have been built in the East Wing, each capable of holding 60 cadets. These are:

The Theatre

The old PT shed has now been converted into a real theatre with raised tiers, a sunken sand model, an orchestral pit and at the back a store room, cloak room, lavatories and a soft drinks bar. This is in addition to the two green rooms and store room built in 1947.

The Laboratories

Two new Laboratories, one for Physics and one for Chemistry with a gas plant, have been constructed on the far side of the canal.

Living Quarters

The old BORs quarters have been converted into officers quarters and six new cycle sheds have been constructed.

The Officers Mess

A new officers mess has just been completed next to Bungalow No. 5 and is to be opened shortly. It consists of a dining hall, a spacious ante-room, a bar and a billiard room.

Playing Fields

One extra football ground has been made on ground formerly belonging to the FRI Golf Course and several BasketBall grounds have been added on ground alongside the Deputy Commandant's Bungalow.

Conclusion

THUS AN OLD TIMER will see many changes when visiting the old IMA, changes which go to the making of a better and more modern institution.

Independence Day Celebrations

15 August 1948

A CEREMONIAL PARADE of Gentlemen Cadets was held on the Academy Parade Ground to celebrate Independence Day – 15 August 1948 – the day on which the people of India regained their heritage of national freedom and sovereign independence after centuries of adverse political vicissitudes.

The Salute was taken by Brigadier Thakur Mahadeo Singh, DSO, the Commandant.

No official invitations were extended on this occasion as there was a garrison parade in Dehra Dun at the same time, and the celebration was restricted to members of the IMA Staff and families, and relations and friends of Gentlemen Cadets.

Unfortunately it rained continuously throughout the celebrations, but this by no means reduced the enthusiasm of the Cadets. It was apparent from their display that they heralded the day with legitimate joy.

The occasion was celebrated in a befitting manner and it brought home to the people watching the parade the real meaning and purpose of the celebrations.

S. P. Malhotra

A Visit to the IMA

By Brig. S. C. Misra
(Formerly Deputy Commandant)

'Memory is the treasure-house of the mind wherein the monuments thereof are kept and preserved'

Fuller

I DO NOT KNOW HOW OTHERS, who have been at the IMA, feel towards that institution, but to me a visit there is like going on a pilgrimage. My last visit has left a lasting impression, which I shall attempt to record in this brief note.

You cannot but have reverence and affection for the IMA, which has almost overnight, in the face of severe handicaps assumed such an important place in our national life. The great leaders – HE Shri Rajagopalachari, Pandit Nehru, Sardar Patel and Sardar Baldev Singh have visited the IMA perhaps more than once since nationalisation, or shall I call it 'transformation', and have carried with them impressions of soldierly efficiency, selfless service based on the teaching of the highest morality which lays down – 'The safety, honour and welfare of your country comes first, always and every time; the honour, welfare and comfort of the men you command comes next; your own ease, comfort and safety comes last always and every time.'

As far as military training went, the IMA always compared most favourably with the world's best military academies. That fine tradition of efficiency has not been lost one whit, and in addition she has become the training ground of the country's leaders, the *Alma Mater*, or the bounteous mother, who will nurture her youth to serve the motherland selflessly.

But let me confine myself to my visit on the occasion of the passing out of the 3rd Regular Course on 11 September 1948 when 185 Gentlemen Cadets received their Regular Commissions. This parade has always been the great annual function of the IMA, but this particular Passing-Out Parade had great significance for all of us. I was naturally thrilled to watch the first product of an all Indian instructional staff, and I had the satisfaction of seeing the finest drill which has been seen for many years.

I for one can vouch that such remarkable precision in the intricate movements of the drill square combined with soldierly carriage and smart turnout has not been seen anywhere else in our country. I shall go further, and say with a feeling of pride that such superb drill will do credit to West Point and Sandhurst.

All the cadets marched past in slow time in close column followed by a march in quick time. They then formed into a square to hear the address of the Defence Minister, after which the Gold Medal (the recent substitute for the sword of honour) was awarded to GC Narindar Singh and the Silver Medal to GC Sowani, both of whom fully deserved these two coveted prizes of the Academy. After the parade the spectators were treated to coffee and light refreshments.

After all these War years the Academy has certainly recaptured much of the old peace-time atmosphere, and brought that institution nearer to the hearts of all Indians. The IMA band played a selection of soft music, and the inspiring strains of the National Anthem could not be forgotten 'long afterwards when it was heard no more'. The dance in Chetwode Hall added greatly to the colour and charm of the occasion, and the band of my regimental centre – the 5th Gurkha Rifles – was in attendance and played the usual jazz tunes.

The Defence Minister.

I feel that the traffic and seating arrangements carried out with meticulous care for details deserve a word of praise. There were about 5,000 spectators (easily the largest gathering which has ever watched a Passing-Out Parade in the IMA) and everybody knew where to go and how to find his own seat.

Personal encomiums must always be avoided, but I cannot help mentioning – Brig. Thakur Mahadeo Singh, the Comdt. and 'Smoky' Malhotra, the Adjutant, who deserve to be congratulated for the first fruit of their labours, which beyond any shadow of a doubt (I shall repeat once again) was of the highest quality. In wishing adieu, I feel very proud indeed of this noble institution of the Nation, and of the achievements of my brother officers who have given their very best in the service of their country, and although the name is now being changed to the Armed Forces Academy I will still say – 'Long live the IMA'.

I do not know when I shall again go on a similar pilgrimage but the memory of the last one will grow richer and give my mind many pleasant joys.

> 'When to the sessions of sweet silent thought, I summon up remembrance of things past –'

Part Three

Inauguration – 4 June 1949

Editorial

THIS TERM WILL ALWAYS BE remembered in the annals of the Academy as Inauguration Term.

On 10 January the Academy reopened as The Armed Forces Academy, the first institution of its kind to train Army, Navy and Air Force Cadets. At Clement Town the Interservice Wing came into being with Col Kamta Prasad as its first Deputy Commandant and Mr Jack Gibson as its first Principal. An article entitled 'The Interservice Wing – Its Start and Prospects,' written by Mr Gibson, appears as a special feature of this the first issue of the AFA Journal.

Also in this issue will be found articles of interest to both Navy and Air Force addicts – 'Navigation in a Nutshell' by Lieut S. H. Sharma, RIN, and 'Old Faithfuls' by F/Lieut D. M. Burjorjee. In addition, the activities of the new Interservice Wing are described in a special Section with photographs to illustrate them.

The Academy has been honoured by many distinguished persons – notably Vice-Admiral W. E. Parry CB, Chief of Naval Staff and Commander-in-Chief, Royal Indian Navy, General K. M. Cariappa OBE, Chief of Army Staff and Commander-in-Chief, Indian Army, and by the Deputy Prime Minister, Sardar Vallabhbhai Patel, who was accompanied by the Hon. Defence Minister, the Hon. Home Minister and the three Services Chiefs. Special Articles on these memorable visits will be found in this issue.

Other activities of interest were the informal visit of General Williams, Engineer-in-Chief, and Dame Emmeline Tanner, formerly Principal of Roedean School, on 9 and 10 January; the Inter University Debating Contest in Chetwode Hall on Saturday, 28 February; the Cadets Dance organised largely by GCs B. S. Bedi and B. S. Irani, and enlivened by a very successful Cadets Band organised by GCs Cameron, Lobo,

Fernandes and Pereira on 9 March; the AFA Flower Show on 20 March, when Capt. A. J. Selvey MBE once again won first prize for the best garden; the visit of the British Debating Team, which gave us a most entertaining debate on Saturday 2 April – Oxford University being represented by Mr Colin Jackson, the leader of the Team, Glasgow University by Mr Jenkins and the University of Wales by Mr McLellan; the visit of a number of GCs from the Military Wing to the Dominion Parliament, New Delhi, on 4 and 6 April; the Inauguration of the AFA Parliament and a very successful Mela at the Military Wing, in which all Corners of India were represented; a number of Concerts, no less than six, for which the Music Circle deserves high praise; the Inter-Company Dramatic Competition, which this year was of a very high order; a very successful Pagal Gymkhana and last and most important the Inauguration Celebrations of 3 and 4 June, 1949.

All the activities were in addition to the routine activities – Camps – Initial and Initiative and Chindit – Banner Matches, Ladies' Guest Nights, both at the Military Wing and the Interservice Wing, and of course, numerous club activities, exhibitions, etc.

The term was marred by two unhappy incidents – one of national importance, the other our personal bereavement – for on 2 March the sudden and tragic death of Mrs Sarojini Naidu, Governor of the United Provinces, was announced to a shocked India – on 29 April the sudden and unexpected death of GC G. S. Chahal of Sangro Company, following an appendicitis operation. Gen. Cariappa, who arrived in Dehra Dun on 29 April, cancelled all his official engagements as a token of respect. Obituary notices in respect of these two tragic incidents appear on another page.

Looking back, this term has been more eventful than any other term since the Academy reverted to its peacetime role. It has lost 3 unforgettable friends – in Lt Col P. S. Bhagat VC, a first class GI, in Col Harbakhsh Singh and Col Mohinder Singh Verdi, two outstanding Deputy Commandants. All of these are to be congratulated on their promotion and new appointments, which they so strongly deserved.

Like Tennyson's *Brook* the Academy can say:

> Men may come and men may go
> but I go on forever

Editor

Deputy Prime Minister's Speech

Inauguration Day, 4 June 1949

SARDAR BALDEV SINGH, and The Commandant, Officers and Cadets of the Armed Forces Academy.

It has given me great pleasure to be present at this inauguration parade of your Academy. The history of this institution illustrates how a small seed very often contains the germ of a future substantial growth. The Indian Military Academy was inaugurated seventeen years ago. It was a most grudging and reactionary policy of Indianisation which was being then put into force, and although the new Academy was hailed as the 'Sandhurst of India', it was merely an inferior and subordinate prototype of that institution. But, as necessity knows no barriers or restrictions, under the heavy stress of war conditions, the scope and purpose of the Academy had to be expanded, as to constitute the training ground for Emergency Commissioned Officers. After the war, the Academy reverted to its previous character, but its whole plan was changed, the moment it was decided by the National Government to found a National War Academy and to set it up here until the Academy could move to a new site.

What was a small establishment some years ago has now blossomed forth into a full-fledged institution, which would be the nursery of great and eminent soldiers of future India. This is an evolution which is merely symbolic of the change that is coming over the entire country after the birth of our independence. During our struggle for Freedom, we infiltrated into many a citadel of the entrenched foreign rulers. The Army, the Air Force and the Navy were, however, the most difficult

Group photograph taken on the occasion of the Inauguration of the Armed Forces Academy, 4 June 1949

Sitting: Lt Col Wright, Asstt Comdt IAEC (MW); Colonel Mohinder Singh Verdi, Deputy Commandant (MW); Brigadier Thakur Mahadeo Singh DSO, Commandant; General K.M. Cariappa OBE, Chief of the Army Staff and C-in-C Indian Army; the Honourable Defence Minister, Sardar Baldev Singh; the Honourable Deputy Prime Minister Sardar Vallabhbhai Patel; Air Marshal Sir Thomas W. Elmhirst KBE, CB, AFC, C-in-C RIAF; Commodore H. Drew CBE, DSC, RN, Deputy C-in-C RIN; Colonel Kamta Prasad MC, Deputy Commandant (ISW); Mr J.T.M. Gibson, Principal ISW.

Standing (1st row): Major Parampal Singh Gill GSO II; Lt Col A.L. Kochhar, Coy Comd (MW); Lt Col E.G. Pettengell MBE, Coy Comd (MW); Lt Col Hartaj Singh, Coy Comd (MW); Lt Col E. Solomon, Admin Officer (MW); Lt Col Budh Singh MC, Senior Instr (MW); Lt Col K.A.S. Raja GSOI (HQ); Lt Col Rajendra Malla, Admin Officer (ISW); Lt Col Baljit Singh, Coy Comd (MW); Lt Col S.K. Korla DSO, MC, Coy Comd (MW); Lt Col R.S.S. Kohli, Coy Comd (MW)

Standing (2nd row): Captain R.S. Pathania, Adjutant (ISW); Lieutenant-Commander D.R. Mehta GSO II (ISW); Squadron/Leader M.B. Chand, Coy Comd (ISW); Major G.S. Saran, Coy Comd (ISW); Captain S.P. Malhotra, Adjutant (MW).

hurdles to cross. Prejudices, which were deep and lasting, an understandable desire not to share with us the secrets of Military warfare, and the policy to keep us militarily weak and untrained were responsible for our slow progress in this sphere. Nevertheless, the last war forced on them the need for a sudden expansion of our Armed Forces, so that at the end of the war, we found our officers and men, who had distinguished themselves on many a field of battle, safely installed in positions of honour, prestige and responsibility. Today, we can boast of an almost completely Indianised Army, Air Force and Navy. Yet, in the same manner as a change has come over us in our other spheres of association with the British, and in the same way as we have welcomed their assistance in other Departments of our activity, we are happy to have amongst us in high and eminent positions, officers of the British Services, who had been lent to us by His Majesty's Government. Let us hope that, with our joint effort, and assisted by their wise counsel, ripe experience and proved ability, we shall evolve the three arms of the Defence Services, which would be worthy of India and protect and uphold the honour, and prestige of the Motherland.

Officers and men of the Academy, you are fortunate in being members of an institution which is unique in the annals of Military History. In no country in the world, has training of all the three Services been centred in one institution. You have, therefore, a wonderful opportunity of developing that inter-wing comradeship and co-ordinated efficiency which would, I am sure, be the envy of other countries. Yours is a truly national institution, in which must grow that healthy secular outlook which is the foundation of true democracy and that unshakable loyalty to the principles on which that democracy must rest. You have traditions of faithful service and devotion to duty, which it would be difficult to find elsewhere. It is up to you to give a solid start to the National War Academy, which would secure its new habitation in the near future. I have no doubt that, rightly led and rightly trained, you will acquit yourselves creditably in every field of military activity. The world is sick unto death of strife; yet, it cannot find its way to peace through violence and armed conflict. While I feel quite certain that the only way in which it can secure a haven of peace and safety is through increasing recognition of the need for settlement of disputes by peaceful and non-violent means, we have to take into account the conditions that exist today. In those conditions, our watch-word must be the scouting motto of 'Be prepared'. It would be for you, Officers

Officers of the IMA – 1949.

and Cadets of the Academy, to translate that watch-word into practice both within the premises of this Academy and outside when you enter upon your duties as full-fledged officers of the Armed Forces of India.

I shall now wish you all God-speed and exhort you to guard the Flag of the Country with your lives and to ensure that neither in word, nor in thought, nor in deed, do you do anything which would bring dishonour to do discredit to that Flag. The smartness of your parade and its efficiency fill me with hope that the protection of our frontiers, the guardianship of our skies and the security of our waters would be safe in your hands. I thank you once more for the opportunity which you have given me of associating myself with this ceremony and assure you that I shall always follow with interest the progress of your institution.

The Interservice Wing, its Start and Prospects

WARFARE IN MODERN TIMES demands the closest possible co-operation between the three Services, co-operation which in the last war was sometimes found to be lacking due to mutual jealousies and lack of understanding between the Services. It is essentially with the idea of putting this right that the Interservice Wing has been started. We do not expect that cadets here will learn the strategy and tactics of combined operations; that they will do later as officers in a combined Staff College; nor will they get anything like a wide or deep experience of the individual problems and customs of the different services; they will have to wait for that till they join their own branch of the Armed Forces; but they will spend two of the formative years of their life in an Interservice atmosphere, in close contact with officers and men of all the Services, and most important of all, for two (and it may be later more) years they will live together, getting to know each other and forming friendships which will overlap the boundaries of the different Services, so that when they separate they will be able to sympathise with the points of view of brother officers in other Services than their own; and when as senior officers they meet each other in Staff conferences they will not start their conferences in an atmosphere tinged with mutual suspicion, but in one enlightened by their previous knowledge of each other and their common experiences and background at the Interservice Wing. It is not over-optimistic to hope that officers who can recall the way they worked together on that scheme along the banks of the Jumna, who played together on that football field at Clement Town, who all remember the eccentricities of old So-and-So when he lectured to them as young cadets, will be in an easier atmosphere, one more fruitful of mutual understanding and co-operation when they meet to discuss their problems, than if they had seen and known little of each other before.

So, in January 1949, the Interservice Wing was started, with the idea that it should benefit from the fine traditions and ripe experience of what had till then been known as the Indian Military Academy, now known as the Military Wing. The two establishments were put under one command and are working in close co-operation, building, we hope, sound foundations for the National War Academy when it is opened at Karakavasla. Obviously we are still in an experimental stage and are still working out what part the different customs of the three Services should play in our life here. When a senior officer enters an Army mess it is the custom for those present to spring to attention. At sea a ship may be rolling, so this is not the custom in the Navy. The Services have different methods of saluting, drilling and dressing. This is to mention only a few of the varied customs and traditions of which the different Services are quite rightly proud, for pride of Service and pride of branch of Service are essential in the build up of keenness and efficiency. How are we to integrate these differences at the Interservice Wing? You cannot have cadets of one institution dressed in different coloured uniforms, marching at different paces and behaving in varied manner, so our formal life here is based mainly upon the Army to which Service the majority of the cadets will go, though as many aspects of the life of the other Services as seem appropriate are brought in. When they join their own Service the cadets will easily make the necessary adjustments in their behaviour. What we are concerned with is to give them a common experience of a smart and efficient way of life, which will be a useful basic training to them wherever they go when they leave us.

Their training here is divided roughly as follows: one part Drill and PT, one part lectures on Service subjects, such as the organisation and history of the different Services, and four parts lectures on academic subjects. In addition, there is time set aside for games, club activities and private study. Our life is thus a combination of that in a cadet training college and that in a university, with the greater part of the time devoted to the university side of life. This is because an officer in these days must have a wide outlook based on a sound education and the ability to think out difficult problems. We hope that when our cadets leave us they will be of at least first class Intermediate standard and in a greater number of subjects than are usually taken in the Intermediate examinations. To achieve this we are collecting an excellent teaching staff and building up first class laboratories, library, model and information rooms. There is wide scope and we hope to find more time for cultural activities outside the lecture halls. We shall soon have adequate playing fields and swimming baths; we have a cinema of our own, where instructional films are regularly shown; there is every facility for PT, boxing and kindred activities; and we already have one of the finest parade grounds in the country. The Interservice Wing has been started with high hopes which the enthusiasm of the cadets and staff gives every promise of bearing fruit of the greatest value.

J. T. M. Gibson

The Army C-in-C's Visit

GENERAL K.M.CARIAPPA OBE, Chief of the Army Staff and Commander-in-Chief, Indian Army, accompanied by Major-General S. B. S. Chimni OBE, Quartermaster General, and Major-General J. H. Wilkinson CIE, Director of Military Training, visited the Armed Forces Academy, Dehra Dun, on 1 and 2 May.

The Commander-in-Chief has a crowded programme in the Station, which included visits to both Wings of the Armed Forces Academy, the Royal Indian Military College, and the Forest Research Institute. Owing to 1 May being a holiday, the Commander-in-Chief could not see the normal training at the Academy, however he addressed all officers and cadets of the Armed Forces Academy in Chetwode Hall.

He said:

General K.M. Cariappa OBE,
C-in-C Indian Army

My talk this morning will be brief because all I want to say to officers and prospective officers is to impress on you the necessity of carrying out orders and instructions instinctively and in the right way.

Cadets, you are being trained here to be officers of Free India's Army. As officers you will have in your hands the lives of the men you command and, therefore, you should set a standard expected of you by the people of the country. You must always be officers and gentlemen. These words, 'officers' and 'gentlemen' mean a lot to you. The traditions of the Army have been built up by our predecessors in the pre-partition Indian Army, and this is a heritage which you should live up to with all sanctity.

There is an age-long saying 'Good Officers, Good Army: Bad Officers, Bad Army'. There are NO bad armies, but the reputation of an Army depends on its officers. These words were said years ago and they are as true today. It is entirely incumbent on you to conduct yourselves as good officers, efficient in the discharge of your service to the country as a whole. You are going to be officers in an Army which is second to none in the world and so you must serve the country and the Government with loyalty, so that this Great Land of Ours progresses to a very high stage in order to take place amongst the Big Powers of the world. Therefore, you must see that India has a really good Army. For this you must be absolutely 100% correct in everything you do, say and write, whether in public, private or any other walk of life.

There is a tendency amongst the people to regard the Army as a money-making career. There is NO place in the Army for people who are after money. Officers in the Army simply make both ends meet. You should not come in the Army if you wish to make money. All that the Army is expected to do is to serve the Government of the Day and to render service to the country with loyalty and unselfishness.

It is absolutely essential that, as officers, you should always be cheerful under all circumstances. The more difficult problems you have to face, the more cheerful you should be as officers.

The other essential qualities required in an officer are described in two words – 'DEEP CUD', standing for DISCIPLINE, ENERGY, ENDURANCE, PERSEVERANCE, COURAGE, UNSELFISHNESS and DETERMINATION.

If you pay attention to each of these qualities, I feel quite certain that it will automatically help you to advance in your profession. The country today needs really good Armed Forces, because in the first month of our Freedom our Armed Forces have risen to great heights and you see the results achieved by them. But for the loyalty, discipline and devotion to duty by the Armed Forces, there would have been a great set-back to our Freedom.

When you pass out as officers, you must pay more attention to the welfare of the men you command than to your own welfare. In old days whenever we got back after a long march of operations, we did not rush to the mess bearer to have drinks. First of all we all used to see if the

> men had their food. Not a single officer went to the mess unless and until he had seen to the comfort of his men first.
>
> You are very fortunate to be brought up on these lines, but always see that you pay attention to the welfare of your men. These days, owing to lack of facilities, quite a number of officers have not had the same fortune of being brought up on the right lines, but, if you find such an atmosphere in your unit when you first join, make sure that you set an example yourself.
>
> On this healthy atmosphere depends the one single factor 'MORALE', on which depends success in war. See that the men you command feel that you are one of them. See that they feel that you do place their comfort before your own. Devote more attention to the men you command. Finally, you should ask yourselves every night whether you have said, done or thought anything that is not worthy of an officer and a gentleman, and if the answer is 'yes', correct it and ensure that the next day it is 'no'. I do not wish to go into more details. That is good enough.

After the address, he inspected the Methods Factory, Library, Information Room and saw the Arts and Crafts Exhibition.

The C-in-C lunched with the cadets of the Interservice Wing and dined with the cadets of the Military Wing, and attended a musical concert.

On 2 May the C-in-C witnessed the pagal gymkhana organised by the cadets of the Academy and gave away the prizes. Next day he gave an informal talk to the ladies of the Academy and entertained them to an ice-cream party.

Admiral Parry's Visit

VICE-ADMIRAL W.E.PARRY CB, Chief of Naval Staff and Commander-in-Chief, Royal Indian Navy, visited Dehra Dun from 16 to 21 March.

On the morning of the seventeenth Admiral Parry inspected Physical Training at the Military Wing. After breakfast with the Commandant he spoke to officers and cadets of the Military Wing, attended a lecture by the Methods Officer, a lecturette by a cadet, a short playlet, and a Current Affairs lecture, after which he gave a second talk to both officers and cadets.

In the evening, after visiting St Dunstan's and the Doon School, Admiral Parry was entertained at the Interservice Wing for drinks and a Buffet Supper.

Vice-Admiral W.E. Parry CB,
C-in-C Royal Indian Navy

On the 18th morning the Naval C-in-C, inspected ISW Cadets on the Drill Square, inspected the quarter guard, visited the MT Lines and gave two talks to the officers and cadets of the Interservice Wing, and lunched in the Cadets Mess.

That evening, having already visited the Royal Indian Military College, he attended a PT Display at the Military Wing given by the Boys of the Jat Regimental Centre, which was followed by the Beating of the Retreat by the Jat Regimental Centre Band, a very pleasing spectacle. Then followed

Dinner in the Cadets Mess, and a special Concert at the Military Wing Theatre.

On Sunday, 20 March, after a brief visit to Mussoorie, Admiral and Mrs Parry witnessed the Finals of the Inter-Unit Athletic Competition, which was won by the Armed Forces Academy Team. Mrs Parry very kindly gave away the prizes.

Command and Staff List Armed Forces Academy – Dehra Dun

Headquarters, AFA

Commandant	Brigadier Thakur Mahadeo Singh DSO, IA
GSO I	Lt Col K. A. S. Raja, The Madras Regiment
GSO II	Major Parmpal Singh Gill RIA

Military Wing

Deputy Comdt	Colonel M. S. Verdi IA
Assistant Comdt, RAEC	Lt Col C. H. E. Wright RAEC
Senior Instructor	Lt Col Budh Singh MC, Indian Grenadiers
Instructor Class 'A'	Lt Col Hartaj Singh RIA
(Coy Comds.)	Lt Col R. S. S. Kohli Indian Grenadiers
	Lt Col E. G. Pettengell MBE, Indian Sigs
	Lt Col Shiv Dayal Singh MC, Jaipur Inf
	Lt Col A. L. Kochhar RIE
	Lt Col Baljit Singh WS, IAC
Admin Officer	Lt Col E. Solomon Raj Rif
GSO II (Fd. Trg.)	Major S. Y. Munshi, Kumaon Regiment
Methods Officer	Major D. M. Kee, 8 GR
Instructor Class 'B' IAEC	Major A. N. Chatterji, Sikh, LI. Attd. IAEC

	Major R. L. Mullick IAEC
	Major V. G. Bapat IAEC
	Major F. S. Patel IAEC
	Major H. R. H. Daniell IAEC
Adjutant	Captain S. P. Malhotra R. Garh, Rif

Interservice Wing

Dy. Comd.	Col Kamta Prasad MC
Adm. Officer	Lt Col Gajendra Malla
GSO II (Trg.)	Lt Comdr. D. R. Mehta RIN
Coy. Comd.	Major G. S. Saran
Coy. Comd.	Sqn./Ldr. M. B. Chand RIAF
Catering Officer	Major H. R. Babbar
GSO III	F/Lt D. M. Burjorjee RIAF
GSO III	Captain A. J. Anand
Adjt.	Captain R. S. Pathania
Asst. AO	F/Lt P. K. Sarkar
P & AO	Captain Hari Singh
PTO	Captain C. S. Bains

The Commandant with the British Staff.

Standing (back row, left to right): WOII W. Paskell, R. Norfolk Regt, S/I C.F. Gatt, APTC, WOII P. Donovan, Middlesex Regt, WOII T. John MM, Welsh Guards, S/I J. Chismon, APTC, WOII L. Pearce, Som LI, WOII J. M. Burke MM, RAC

Standing (centre row): S/I R.D. Greenwood, APTC, WOI L.A. Lord RAC, S/I L. Fairey APTC, WOII J. Armstrong RSF, WOII W. Cheater, Gloucester Regt, S/I W. Jones, APTC

Sitting (left to right): WOII M.E. Hill, E. Yorks, WOII W. Burrows, APTC, RSM G.S. Hutchinson MM, R. Lincolns (Military Wing), Commandant, RSM S. Prestidge, R. Warwicks (ISW), WOII F. Arnott, Royal Scots, WOII E. Waud, Black Watch

Autumn Term, 1949

Editorial

THIS YEAR HAS SEEN THE BIRTH and death of an institution. On 1 January 1949, The Armed Forces Academy officially came in to being; on 31 December it officially lost its entity. But what's in a name? The Academy lives on under its new title of The National Defence Academy.

The most notable event of the term was the well-deserved promotion of our Commandant to the rank of Major-General. This honour is shared by all – staff and cadets – we congratulate Major-General Mahadeo Singh and Mrs Mahadeo Singh, whose share in the honour is no less.

We have been fortunate this term in the variety of official and non-official visitors. The services have been well represented both from home and abroad.

Air Marshal
Sir Thomas Elmhirst KBE, CB,
AFC, C-in-C Royal
Indian Air Force.

On 12 and 13 October Commodore H. Drew, Deputy C-in-C, Royal Indian Navy, Commodore H. N. S. Brown, Officer Commanding, Royal Indian Naval Squadron and Commodore H. B. Ellison, Director of Naval Training visited both the Military Wing and the Interservice Wing.

On 20 October we were honoured by a visit from His Excellency Sir Homi Modi, Governor of the United Provinces, which is reported on in a special article.

On 7 November Mr G. D. Sondhi,

Lt Gen. (now Sir) Dudley Russell.

Deputy Director, All-India Radio and well-known educationist, was our guest.

Another interesting visit was that of Colonel Divisionnaire. Dr Karl Brunner, of the Swiss Army, which is reported on elsewhere.

On 25 November General Sant Singh, Commanding 4th Indian Division, presented the Academy with a magnificent trophy in the form of the Divisional Eagle at a Dinner given in his honour. A short article on this memorable event is also published in this issue.

Then came Lt Gen. R. N. Gale, Director General of Military Training from the War Office, who visited the Academy on 28 November.

On 3 December Col C. T. E. Collins DWE, accompanied by his GI Lt Col W. G. Riley, paid us a visit.

Finally at the Passing-Out Parade of the Fourth Course were honoured by the presence of Air Marshal Sir Thomas Elmhirst, C-in-C, RIAF. A full article on this distinguished officer's visit is reported on in a special article in this issue.

So another term and another year draw to their close. With the New Year comes another notable change, not only in the Academy but in the country itself, for on 26 January 1950, India becomes a republic. It is only appropriate therefore that with the birth of a nation the Academy takes on the new designation of The National Defence Academy. Long may they both prosper.

Dr Karl Brunner's Visit

A NOTABLE OCCASION was the visit of Dr Karl Brunner, Colonel Divisionnaire of the Swiss Army, who paid a 3 day visit to the Academy from 21 to 23 November.

On the night of the twenty-first the Swiss General dined in the Cadets' Mess at the Military Wing and delivered an inspiring speech.

On the morning of the twenty-second Dr Karl Brunner inspected the Military Wing Cadets on parade and was very favourably impressed with their drill and turn-out.

Then followed a tour of the Chetwode Building including a visit to

The Military Wing Parade.

the lecture halls, Information Room, Library, etc., after which he visited Camp Initiative and had lunch in Camp. Returning to the Miliary Wing, Dr Karl Brunner watched the cadets playing games, before going on to the Commandant's House for tea.

In the evening the Swiss General dined with the Officers and Staff the Interservice Wing.

On the morning of the twenty-third a tour of the Interservice Wing was made, followed by lunch in the Cadets' Mess.

Thus ended a very delightful visit. All were greatly impressed by the keen interest the Colonel Divisionnaire took in everything he saw, and it is hoped that he took away as favourable an impression of us as we had of him.

The Presentation of the Eagle

Gen. Sant Singh's Visit

MAJOR-GENERAL SANT SINGH, Commander 4th Division, visited the Academy on 25 November 1949, together with his GI, Lt Col S. S. Malik, and was entertained at a dinner given in his honour in the Cadets' Mess.

On this historic occasion Major-General Sant Singh in an after dinner

The presentation of the Eagle.

speech said that the 'Fighting Fourth' the premier division of the Indian army, had decided to present the Academy with a Trophy in the form of the Divisional Eagle – 'The Symbol of Determination, Strength and Vigilance, the three vital essentials of soldiering'.

He said that this institution was nearest to their hearts and that the 4th Division wished to be the first to link its name with the Academy under its new name the Armed Forces Academy.

After these inspiring words the General called upon Wing SUO Himmeth Singh to accept the gift from all ranks of the Fourth Infantry Division.

The trophy is to be awarded to the best Company in Endurance and Physical efficiency, indicating the spirit of the Eagle.

Sir Homi Modi's Visit

On 20 October the Academy was honoured by a visit from His Excellency The Governor of the UP, Sir Homi Modi.

The visit though short was a memorable one and will be particularly remembered for the intimacy with which the Governor spoke to all and for the delightful humour that emanated from his lips.

His Excellency was only able to spare the Military Wing an hour and in that short time he visited Chetwode Hall, the Museum, the Library, the Information Room, the Methods Factory and two or three instructional periods, of which the Cadets discussion on The Language Problem was commented on very favourably.

After a visit to the Playing Fields His Excellency drove to the Interservice Wing where he carried out a similar tour, including a visit to the Cadets' Quarters, the New Parade Ground, and the Officers' Mess.

In the evening the Governor honoured the Academy by dining in the Cadets' Mess at the Military Wing.

The Fourth Course Passes Out

THE FINAL and most spectacular event of the term was the End of Term Parade followed by various functions both outdoor and indoor.

On this occasion the Academy was honoured by the presence of Air Marshall Sir Thomas Elmhirst, C-in-C, RIAF, who was accompanied by Lady Elmhirst and Lady Cunningham. Among the high ranking officers who attended the parade were Lt Gen. (now Sir) Dudley Russell, Lt Gen. Master, Maj. Gen. Wilkinson, Maj. Gen. T Sheo Dutt Singh and Air Vice-Marshall Mukherjee.

Addressing the cadets the Air Marshall said, 'It is a great honour to belong to the Armed Forces. The main requirements of a Service career are character, loyalty, discipline, leadership and devotion to duty.'

'Without loyalty and discipline,' he added, 'the Armed Forces is a rabble. When it comes under fire in difficult circumstances it is loyalty and discipline that holds it together and makes it a worthy force.

He stressed the necessity of efficient leadership and advised cadets not to marry before they were 25, since it was not possible for young officers to be efficient officers and efficient husbands at the same time. He therefore advised young officers not to marry until they attained the substantive rank of Captain.

The presentation of the Banners, which followed, was an impressive spectacle. Kohima Company, the champion company, received the King George V Banner, and Cassino Company, the best company in team games, received the Governor-General's Banner.

The Sword of Honour, which has recently been reintroduced, was then presented to Wing SUO Himmeth Singh, the best all-round cadet, the Gold Medal to SUO Sodhi, for standing first in order of merit, a Silver Medal to SUO K. V. Raghavan, for standing second, and a Silver

Medal to SUO V. M. Sundaram, for standing first in order of merit in the 2nd Technical Graduates Course.

On this great occasion, after an impressive parade, 180 cadets of the Fourth Course and 35 cadets of the 2nd Technical Graduates Course received their commissions.

Coffee and refreshments in Chetwode Hall regaled the successful cadets and the parents after the parade and gave them an opportunity to meet the distinguished visitors.

Then followed a PT Display by both Gentlemen Cadets and the PT Staff after which lunch was served on the terraces.

After lunch a cricket match between the Commandant's XI versus The Rest was played, in which the Commandant's XI won by a small margin.

Tea was then served on the terraces followed by the Beating of the Retreat by the Academy Band and Pipers.

At night a very successful farewell party was held in Chetwode Hall, and on the chime of midnight Air Marshal Sir Thomas Elmhirst presented each successful cadet with his 'pips'. With the presentation of the last 'pips' the lights went out and when they went on again 215 new officers were wearing the badges of their rank.

Thus ended a most eventful day, the Fourth Course singing their song *We hate to leave.*

Message from the C-in-C

To the Cadets Passing Out from the Military Wing of the Armed Forces Academy, on 10 December 1949

TODAY YOU ARE PASSING OUT as trained Cadets to get your Commissions in the normal manner. I congratulate you all on the successful termination of your course at this Academy.

Remember, you are coming into an Army which has a very high tradition and in which you will have the great honour and privilege of commanding some of the finest men in the world. As officers, you belong to a class above the common level of life because you have the proud privilege of serving the country as soldiers and as soldiers you have the opportunity of making every kind of sacrifice, even to the extent of giving your lives in the battlefield, in the service of country. I want you all to start off your life as officers with the highest standard possible in everything you do. You MUST pay the greatest attention to the minutest detail in your work, i.e. you must be thorough in everything you do. See that you set an example to the men you command in your turn-out, in your behaviour, in your efficiency as a soldier and in various other essential factors of life which to make one a good citizen of the country.

We in the Army are the custodians of the tax-payers' property. I have said so many times before. This property consists of men, material, accommodation and supplies of all kinds in the Army. You, as officers, will be in charge of all these at various times and I want you to see that you discharge this sacred trust placed in your hands by the people of our country as officers of our Army, loyally, honestly, truthfully and with the highest standard of integrity.

Your profession is indeed a very noble one. Your work in the Army will be starting when you are permitted to wear your first Star, and it will go on increasing more and more as time goes on. You must never 'let up'. The time you may waste in peace in useless pursuits you will pay for in 'blood' in war, for the lives of men you will command will be in your hands at all times. You MUST read widely and educate yourselves professionally as soldiers and also equip yourselves with adequate knowledge of the country in general so as to enable you to carry out your second important duty to the country, i.e. as a citizen of the land. You serve the country as Indians, as INDIANS always. Never allow the virus of communalism to enter in to the Army under any circumstances.

One of the most important matters which I want everyone of you to pay attention to, besides the professional efficiency of yourselves and the men you command, is the happiness and the contentedness of the men you command, which is generally known as the 'welfare of the troops'. Our men are magnificent. They are absolute gems. See that they have full confidence in your ability to train them in peace and lead them in war, and at the same time, have such faith in your personal interest in their welfare generally, which includes their feeding, clothing, housing, pay and allowances, promotions, leave, and last but not least, their domestic problems. Get to know your men really well. Take a personal interest in their welfare. Make them feel that although you may be very hard on them on parade, you are most kind to them in their welfare matters off-parade. The 'Jawan' will respect you for this and will follow you anywhere. Be always correct and proper in your behaviour, in your turn-out, both in private and in public. Be as courteous as you possibly can to civilians of all grades, because, remember, we are today the people's Army and we do want them to realise that we are there to serve them whilst we, as soldiers, must keep a certain degree of aloofness, merely to ensure that we maintain discipline and NOT get 'mixed up' with party politics which might be detrimental to the loyalty and efficiency of the Army. Go ahead. There is nothing impossible to a determined man.

I wish you the best of luck.'

Sd./- K. M. CARIAPPA
General
Commander-in-Chief.

The Hindustani Majlis

THE HINDUSTANI MAJLIS has been started with the object of promoting the understanding and appreciation in cadets of Indian customs, culture and its literature of the Hindustani language. To this end, a library of classical books in the two main Indian languages Hindi and Urdu, has been formed.

The inauguration of the Majlis on 23 October 1946 was marked by great enthusiasm and keenness on the part of all members. The meeting was historic in the sense that for the first time in the life of the Academy, thoughts on Indian culture and literature were expressed in Hindustani.

Another meeting of the Majlis was held on 20 December 1946 on the occasion of HE the C-in-C's visit. Individual views expressed on the subject of 'What I understand by Indian culture' gave excellent material for thought and practice in the future. The recitation of Urdu and Hindi poems by cadets in period costumes and finally a farewell to the outgoing cadets ended a very successful term.

Random Notes

After many years of devoted service, Miss L. Lyall MBE, the matron of the IMA hospital, is shortly to leave the IMA. She will be greatly missed by staff and cadets alike. We offer our sincerest good wishes for her future happiness with Colonel W. A. Asher, RAEC.

Our congratulations go to GC Bhalla and GC K. K. Kaul who, for outstanding merit over the whole ten months of their cadetships, were awarded the Sword of Honour and the Silver Medal respectively.

The successes of GC S. W. Burrett and GC E. Thomas in the Dehra Dun Olympic Games are worthy of special mention. Burrett, having won the mile race, proceeded to win the nine-mile marathon in the record time of 51 mins. 9 secs. Thomas won the trophy for the best athlete; being first in the broad and high jumps, and in putting the shot, and second in throwing the javelin.

The high spot of the earlier part of the term was the visit of Major General D. C. Hawthorn CB, DSO, Director of Military Training who took the salute at a Battalion parade on 21 November 1946 and inspected field and academic training.

Naushahra Company

IN ORDER TO ACCOMMODATE THE 7th Course a new Company was raised in June 1949. This Company was named NAUSHAHRA after the heroic battle of Naushahra. Ours was the first Company to be raised after the IMA became the AFA, and the first Company to be named after a battle fought by free Indians on Indian soil. This gave us a better background and better traditions to work up to, at the start.

The nucleus of our Company was formed from 4th, 5th and 6th Course Cadets coming from various Companies. But it is amazing how quickly we built our traditions and company spirit. It was our immense good luck to have Lieut-Colonel Hoshiar Singh, IOM, IDSM, as our Company Commander. We had to wait for him but we all today think it is worth while waiting for such a Company Commander, even if we have to wait for ages.

In the 'Battle-for-Blocks', Naushahra was given a good start in the GG and the KGV Banners. The final results are yet for time to decide but whatever the outcome Naushahrians can easily look back on their first term with triumph and satisfaction. Whether we won or lost was not what mattered with Naushahrians. Like Olympian maxims Naushahra was inspired more by the spirit of healthy competition than the momentary pleasure of winning. All those who saw Naushahra in action either in the Swimming Pool, on the PT fields, at the Volley Ball nets or the football grounds, will bear me out when I say we took both our triumphs and our losses with a smile – typical and characteristic of Naushahrian spirit.

We have another peculiarity – ours is the only Company which has arranged two social functions in a term and we expect to have a third one before the close of the term. These social functions not only brought us together, but also built in us a sense of unity and made it a habit with us to act as a family – our Ante-room-procedure was a joy – when routine orders were over and time permitted. We enjoyed and applauded either some wholesome humour or divine music as in a family-sitting-room. Ours was a life of informal formality and unimposed discipline. We have had our own achievements – the IV, V & VI Courses came second in the Drill Competition, and the VI Course came first in Camp Chindit – but our greatest achievement is the feeling, which we have treasured about our great Company, and the fact that if anything is ever to remain green in our memories about our life in the AFA, it is the memory of these days which we spent in Naushahra. On behalf of all of us who are passing out of this place, I give my heartiest good wishes to our successors. Keep the spirit of Naushahra alive and make it an ideal, a novel ideal.

B. P. Upasani

Rugby

In September, Rugby Football was re-introduced in the AFA. While some cadets had played Rugger before, to many the game was entirely new. But there was plenty of enthusiasm and keenness to learn the game, within four weeks of training two formidable packs were formed, and with the abundance of fleet-footed cadets, there was not difficulty in finding fast three-quarters. Two teams were formed and six matches were played before the close of the season.

It was the hope of every cadet that an Academy Rugby XV would be formed. But due to the short season of training and also due to the little experience of most players, this was not possible.

The success of the season was mainly due to Lt Colonel C. H. E. Wright who took a very keen interest in the game. On every practice evening he was on the field teaching the newcomers, not only the rules of the game, but also how to play it. His co-worker was Major P. B. Srivastava, who trained the forwards and the three-quarters. The task of forming the packs was entrusted to RSM Burke. We are especially indebted to him and CSM Waud for coming all the way from Clement Town to teach and coach the Rugby enthusiasts.

In conclusion, it is hoped that next season a strong AFA Rugby XV will be formed and we also hope that Rugby football will find its place as one of the major games in the AFA.

G. Clifton,
Sangro.

Aero Club

THE AERO CLUB of the Interservice Wing started functioning in February 1949 under the guidance of Sqn. Ldr. M B. Chand.

The object of the club is to make the cadets air-minded and to encourage the study of Aeronautical Engineering and to start model aircraft building and flying.

At the first meeting which was held in February 1949 the following cadets were appointed office-bearers:

Cadet A. K. Lahiri	President
Cadet S. K. Dey	Secretary
Cadet S. Roy	Members of the Executive Committee
Cadet P. C. Dubey	
Cadet P. P . Avasthi	

The club proved to be quite popular and over 60 cadets joined as initial members. Despite difficulties regarding modelling equipment and proper working facilities, quite a bit of spadework was put in during the 1st Term. Lectures on the Theory of Flight and the parts of Modern Aeroplanes proved quite informative, and an air-minded atmosphere was introduced by bringing in various magazines, aerial photographs, and maps.

In the second term Aero Modelling was started on a firm footing. At first only section *kits* were assembled and flown. Then, later on, solid models were constructed and a few gliders were even made.

Next term the club hopes to start manufacturing flying models. The workshop has also been expanded and the club has secured two rooms for its own use.

The lectures of the 2nd Term were of a more advanced nature, especially the ones about Wireless Aids to Navigation and Airmanship. Thirteen members of the club will be going to the 'All-India Aero Modellers' Rally, Calcutta' during this winter break to witness the Rally.

Births and Marriages

BIRTHS. We congratulate:
Maj. & Mrs F. Shergill – on the birth of a son.
Capt. & Mrs H. S. Chandele – on the birth of a son.

MARRIAGES. We congratulate:
Capt. Mohi Mohan Bose, the Bihar Regiment, on his marriage to Biyoya, daughter of Mr and Mrs P. C. Chowdhri of Lucknow, on Saturday 24 December 1949 at Calcutta.
Maj. R. L. Mullick IAEC (who left us recently) on his marriage to Lalita, daughter of the late Mr Dewan Chand Sethi and Mrs Sethi on Sunday 11 December 1949, at Dehra Dun.

PROMOTIONS. We congratulate:
Maj. Gen. Thakur Mahadeo Singh DSO, on his promotion to Major-General's rank.
Maj. S. P. Malhotra and Maj. Gurbaksh Singh on attaining their majority.
Dr Virendra Verma, on his promotion from Lecturer to Reader.

Editorial Staff

Chief Editor	Lt Col C. H. E. Wright
Assist. Editors	Lt Comdr T. E. De Almeida, IN
	Major R. Som Dutt
	Mr T. N. K. Rayan
	Mr S. S. Mathur

Part Four

Indian Military Academy: The Cradle of Military Leadership

By Lt Gen. V. P. Gupta

Introduction

THE INDIAN MILITARY ACADEMY (IMA) turns sixty-four years on 10 December 1996 and is the archetypal military institution in the whole of the Indian sub-continent. It is the first training institution of its kind in the region established with a view to inducting Indian Officers in the British Indian Army which was then mainly officered by the English. The training in this premier establishment has been associated with blood, fire and fury. It is therefore, natural that the training of gentlemen cadets, viz Officer trainees is multifaceted and multiform – an action filled scenario embracing both mind and body. The pace of training is fast and intense. Self-esteem, the sense of honour, development of character qualities, training in professionally relevant functional skills as also development of the creative and critical faculties of the trainees are some of the chosen areas of training. In order to achieve the aim of training, the curriculum has been developed by experts and specialists. To ensure that training objectives do not stagnate or become monotonous the syllabus is subjected to periodic review and revision, updating it to meet the emerging professional requirements of the Army, arising from changing security perspective and defence imperatives. The present syllabus came into effect in January 1993.

As part of the character building, all thoughts and actions of the trainees are guided by a very demanding Honour code System, which is directed at improving the personal value system of the Gentlemen Cadets so that a healthy blend of the individual and societal objectives are achieved.

The Campus

THE LUSH GREEN FORESTS and rugged beauty of the Shivaliks on one side and the majestic splendour of the Himalayas on the other make the Indian Military Academy an ideal locale for training young men in the art of warfare. The campus has grown over the years and is divided into two geographical sections called the North Campus and South Campus with the Chakrata road from Dehra Dun to the hill resort of Shimla bisecting the two. The main complex named after Field Marshal Sir Philip Chetwode, the then Commander-in-Chief in India during 1932, has become an integral part of the History of the IMA. The building was initially built in 1930 for the Railway Staff College. It was then called Dormer Hall. The architecture of the building resembles that of the 'Hall of Middle Temple' in England. It

Chetwode building today.

was acquired for the IMA during 1931 and was christened Chetwode Hall, and was used for all formal and informal functions like opening and closing addresses of new courses, addresses by visiting dignitaries, Inter Battalion Debates and the Pipping Ceremony. Since the strength of the passing-out courses is large and Academy cannot be accommodated inside the Chetwode Hall, all these functions now take place in the Khetarpal Auditorium. The Chetwode Hall at present houses the IMA Museum.

During the early stages, the campus grew contiguous to the Chetwode Building. With the finalisation of the Zonal plan in 1962, the process of construction started in a planned manner. Some of the major training and administrative facilities which have come up as part of the Key Location Plan include an Olympic size Swimming Pool, inaugurated in 1970 and named after Capt GS Salaria – recipient of the nation's highest gallantry award 'Param Vir Chakra' in 1961, a sprawling sports complex with an impressive stadium called Somnath Stadium, again named after another Maj. Somnath Sharma 'Param Vir Chakra'. An imposing auditorium was built in 1982 and named Khetarpal Auditorium after Lt Arum Khetarpal – one of the alumni of the Academy who was awarded 'Param Vir Chakra' during the Indo-Pak War of 1971. The Auditorium has a seating capacity of 1,487, including a balcony seating of 500.

Training Facilities

MODERN TEACHING AIDS systems like projection Television (PTV), Computers and a Close Circuit Television (CCTV) are available in all classrooms. An Officers Mess and accommodation for faculty including officers and other ranks have been built. Each Gentleman Cadet has his own room, a comfortable retreat where he can relax. Living conditions are designed akin to those found in a Officers Mess. Ante-rooms have been tastefully furnished for their relaxation/recreational activities.

6. An elaborately prepared Master Plan caters for the growth and development of the IMA Estate in keeping with anticipated needs of the twenty-first century.

7. The Academy Library, which had just 800 books initially, has now about one lakh. In recent years it has expanded and diversified its services. The most significant development has been the establishment

of Battalion and Company Libraries with a view to providing the Gentlemen Cadets with easy access to reading material.

Organisation and Re-organisation

SINCE THE DAY of its inception, when the Academy had a humble beginning with an intake of only 40 cadets (of which 10 belonged to erstwhile State Forces) during each term, the strength of the Academy rose to a one time high during the days of national emergency in the sixties when 3,632 Gentlemen Cadets passed out from its portals. Since 1965, the Academy has settled down to its routine of training for permanent Regular Commission officers numbering about 1,200 at any one time. The Army Cadets College located at Pune in Maharashtra, the progeny of the Kitchener College Nowgong, became a feeder wing of the Academy when it shifted to Dehra Dun in 1977. The scale of the Academy's operations can be gauged from the fact that in 63 years of its existence, about 40,000 Cadets have been commissioned from this glorious Institution.

Reflecting the changes sweeping across the country in general and the army in particular is the posting of Women Officers as Instructors

Nizam Pavilion.

in the Academic Department of the Academy. A batch of such instructors was posted in 1993 and as of today there are six Women Officers on the staff of the Academy, all belonging to the Army Educational Corps (AEC).

Curricular and Co-curricular Activities

THE AIM OF TRAINING is to develop the qualities of leadership in all Gentlemen Cadets. The theoretical aspects are taught through 'Integrated General Leadership Training' capsule, whereas practical aspects are developed through example and practice. The trainees are put in Command of Section and Platoons during tactical exercises and as rotatory appointments at the Academy. They are trained in refereeing and umpiring of games and organisation of adventurous activities, entertainment programmes under the general guidance of members of the staff.

During the last 15 years, the training has become more pragmatic, innovative and need-based. The training for leadership role including development of character qualities and human value system has gained primacy in all its facets. Physical fitness, excellence in games and sports and adventure training get primary place in the training schedule.

The syllabus is based on the tactical handling of an infantry Platoon and co-operation with other arms. Therefore, irrespective of the Corps or Regiment in to which the Gentlemen Cadet is Commissioned, he is trained as an Infantry Platoon Commander, as it is felt that he is first and foremost a soldier who must be prepared to lead his men in battle. Subjects like Tactics, Map Reading, Weapon Training, Organisation and Administration, Field Engineering, Radio Telephony, Intelligence and Security, Military Law and Regimental Accounts etc, are taught covering both theoretical and practical aspects.

Academic training which includes Foundational Professional Studies is an integral part of the total training package needed for professional development of the Gentlemen Cadets. Subjects like Science and Warfare, Computer Application, Military History, Military Geography, Military Psychology & Ethics, Management, Communication Skills, Current Affairs and International Relations are taught to the Gentlemen Cadets as part of this package.

In order to inculcate healthy pursuits, indoor and outdoor clubs have

Khetarpal Auditorium.

ben revamped. Arts and Painting, Photography, Computer Application, Science and Technology, Music, Dramatics, and the Literary Societies provide ample scope to the Gentlemen Cadets to develop their potential and pursue hobbies and interests. Outdoor Clubs which are adventure orientated include Hiking and Trekking, Angling, River Rafting, Para-Sailing, Cycling, Mountaineering, Shooting, Riding, Polo and Golf.

Conclusion

NINETEEN NINETY SIX is a special year for the Indian Military Academy – special because the One Hundredth Regular course commenced on 11 January. We have come a long way since our inception in 1932 and in the process has developed customs, procedures and traditions that have evolved over the years keeping in tune with our special role and requirements. By the time a Gentlemen Cadet has completed his course here, he would already have had enough confidence to move on to the more specialised life of his chosen allotted Corps or Regiment.

No organisation can afford to be static – this is true for the IMA also. Amidst the change and evolution, one thing has remained constant and given us a unique and singular character – this is the core values epitomised by our Chetwodian Credo:

THE SAFETY, HONOUR AND WELFARE OF YOUR COUNTRY COME FIRST, ALWAYS AND EVERY TIME;

THE HONOUR, WELFARE AND COMFORT OF THE MEN YOU COMMAND, COME NEXT;

YOUR OWN EASE, COMFORT AND SAFETY COME LAST, ALWAYS AND EVERY TIME.

Commandants of the Indian Military Academy

1.	Brig L. P. Collins CB, DSO, OBE, ADC	1932–36
2.	Brig H. E. W. S. Kingsley CIB, DSO, ADC	1936–39
3.	Brig K. D. E. L. Young MC	1939–42
4.	Brig J. K. Jones DSO	1942–44
5.	Brig A. B. Barltrop OBE, MC	1944–47
6.	Brig T. H. Mahadeo Singh DSO	1947–48
7.	Maj. Gen. T. H. Mahadeo Singh DSO	1949–50
8.	Maj. Gen. K. S. Thimayya DSO	1950–51
9.	Maj. Gen. M. S. Wadalia	1951–53
10.	Brig E. Habisullah	1953–54
11.	Brig A. P. J. I. Randhir Singh	1954–56
12.	Brig M. M. Khanna MVC	1956–58
13.	Brig Gobinder Singh	1958–59
14.	Brig N. D. Nahavati MC	1960–62
15.	Brig P. S. Bhagat VC	1962–63
16.	Maj. Gen. S. C. Pandit VrC	1963–64
17.	Maj. Gen. K. Zorawa Singh MC	1964–66
18.	Maj. Gen. J. T. Sataravala MBE, MC	1966–67
19.	Maj. Gen. D. K. Palit VrC, 1967–69	
20.	Maj. Gen. Rajendra Prasad	1969–72
21.	Maj. Gen. I. C. Katoch	1972–74
22.	Maj. Gen. B. R. Prabhu	1974–75
23.	Maj. Gen. S. C. Sinha	1975–76
24.	Maj. Gen. G. S. Rawat PVSM, AVSM	1976–79

25.	Maj. Gen. Rajendra Nath PVSM	1979–80
26.	Lt Gen. M. Thomas PVSM, AVSM, VSM	1980–83
27.	Lt Gen. Himmeth Singh PVSM	1983–84
28.	Lt Gen. B. B. Sengal PVSM	1984–86
29.	Lt Gen. S. S. Brar	1986
30.	Lt Gen. V. P. Gupta	1986–89
31.	Lt Gen. N. P. S. Bal PVSM	1989–90
32.	Lt Gen. Y. S. Tomar PVSM	1990–91
33.	Lt Gen. M. A. Zaki PVSM, AVSM, VrC	1991
34.	Lt Gen. J. C. Pant AVSM	1991–94
35.	Lt Gen. Inder Varha AVSM	1994
36.	Lt Gen. Amarjit Sandhu	1996–

Appendices

Appendix I

The Partition of India

Letter from Lt Gen. M. Attiqur Rahman describing his journey with refugees from Dehra Dun to Pakistan after Partition.

He was the leader of the convoy transporting Muslims from the refugee camps he had set up at the IMA. At that time he was a major and was responsible for both army personnel and civilians.

THE PARTITION OF INDIA came as a surprise to many of us who were either in a theatre of war overseas, or had taken little or no part in local politics. The even tenor of life at the IMA was shaken.

I happened to be the seniormost officer at the IMA who was leaving for Pakistan. A partition committee was formed at the IMA of which Mahadeo Singh and I were members and Inder Gill was the very efficient secretary. We were also responsible, I think, for the RIMC.

Anyway we divided all the assets of the IMA both movable and immovable on a ratio of 2 to 1.

Somewhere along the line I was asked to organise a camp for Muslims who had fled from some communal rioting in Dehra Dun (and I suppose in the surrounding countryside).

We were given some barracks nearby and we started them off. I do not think there were many persons in the camp say about 200 or so. I do not know what happened to these. Some dispersed on their own but some we took on the train with us.

You will perhaps recall that the personnel who were due for Pakistan left in two main parties. Officers and Cadets by air and the residual by train.

I was in charge of the train party. It was composed of many bogies both for passengers and our heavy gear. The left over cadets from the RIMC and the IMA came with us. In addition the ex-Royal Families of Afghanistan who had been given shelter by the British over the many years in Dehra Dun had almost half the train and a few bogies were allotted to the Tac School (I think).

A very grouchy British Officer with a few men went along for our protection. The poor old British Officer did not fully comprehend the change that was taking place in the subcontinent and complained about the drinking water and the undisciplined crowd on the platform etc. Nor frankly did many of us understand it all either.

Even I as the OC train, did not know as to which route we were going to take to the new country of Pakistan. We were all guessing that we would make a dash for Lahore via Amritsar.

Mahadeo Singh and some others came to see us off at the railway station. It was very nice of them indeed. The next morning we found ourselves in Delhi. We were quite comfortable for waiters from the Station gave us our meals and our water tanks were refilled etc.

The train eventually left Delhi for Bombay and by and large we had little excitement on the way except once when we stopped at a wayside Station and some armed civilians were asking the railway authorities as to the composition of the train. When they were duly informed they left in a couple of cars and we apprehended some mischief on the way.

We alerted our protection party and all of us who had weapons were told to man the windows. However nothing happened throughout the night though we were happy to reach the cosmopolitan city of Bombay.

In Bombay we were taken to the Kalyan Transit Camp and my only memory of this place was that of an old lady in our room who snored heavily and loudly throughout the night.

Eventually we were loaded on to a ship for Karachi. I was again for my sins, made OC Ship.

I recall that I did a tour of the below deck accommodation to see the arrangements for the ORs. I was surprised to find some 20–30 Western type of Women in Western dress including hats in a group together. All around this group were the ORs milling around trying to find somewhere to lie down.

I later found out that the ladies were married in Italy and elsewhere to Sepoys and were travelling rather uncomfortably with them to Pakistan.

After about 3–4 days we arrived in Karachi from Bombay and were met by a band on the quay and our journey from Dehra Dun was over.

Appendix II

A Memorable Day at the IMA

THE STORY I AM ABOUT TO RELATE took place on Sunday 1 April 1934 when I was a Gentleman Cadet.

On Saturday 31 March it was decided to play an April Fool prank on our Officers and the Deputy Commandant in particular, who was officiating Commandant in the absence of Brig. Collins, our Commandant. The Deputy Commandant, who had a very quick temper, was the least revered of our Officers but he was a very religious man, who attended church regularly every Sunday with his family.

Our campaign was to sabotage his efforts to go to church on All Fools Day, as we thought we could get away with it on such an occasion. At midnight we forgathered on the parade ground. Here in front of Chetwode Building stood two draught cannon of the First World War vintage. By sheer weight of numbers we pulled them out of their setting and dragged them along the metalled road and dumped one in front of the Dy Comdt's gate. We were afraid that the noise we created would awaken the dead, but fortune favoured us. We realised that the Dy Comdt would probably be the first to notice this untoward obstruction in front of his gate as he went to Church with his family dressed in their Sunday best, and fly into one of his uncontrollable frenzies and we wickedly wished nothing better.

To make assurance doubly sure we took the precaution to dump the other gun in front of the Adjutant's gate. In addition the heavy steel marine mines in front of Chetwode Buildings we managed to roll, for they were hollow, in front of the Main Gate of the Academy. Add to this we flung sports gear all over the playing fields, removed pictures and paintings in Chetwode Hall, stopped the Academy clock at twelve o'clock, laid out fire-fighting equipment ready for action and placed the high hurdles on the roof of the Main Building. Even electric danger signs displayed on electric transformers were removed and stuck on the name plates of the not-so-popular officers of the Staff.

Imagine the consternation of the Dy Comdt when having risen early and assembled his family in their Sunday best, ready for departure to church, only to find a vintage cannon blocking his egress. Fuming like the traditional general in a Bateman cartoon, he sent for the Adjutant, who lived next door. The unfortunate Adjutant found his gateway also blocked, so hurried on foot to report to the Dy Comdt who ordered him to sound an alarm bell to summon all cadets.

The GCs awaiting such a signal, assembled and doubled to the Dy Comdt's bungalow where they were told in no uncertain terms to put everything back where it belonged within an hour without fail, after which they were ordered to assemble in Chetwode Hall for the officiating commandant's address. Here they were harangued and told it had been a stupid action on their part for April Fool was essentially an English custom and that they had misbehaved, undermining the discipline of the Academy. As a result they were confined to barracks until further notice and that at two o'clock that afternoon there would be a ceremonial parade under the Adjutant, whom we called 'the fire-eater', because of his emitting fire on the drill square. This we took in our stride for we were overjoyed at the success of our escapade.

Five minutes before the time, as was our wont, we were fallen in on the concrete drill square, dressed in khaki drill, while the fire-eater sauntered on parade in his ceremonial dress – khaki drill jacket, tartan breeches and black leather top boots with spurs. We gloated over his discomfort, forgetting our own. The Dy Comdt, to our delight, was equally suffering from the heat. The drill lasted a full hour and as cadets I don't think we ever drilled better, such was our elation. The next day a repetition, but on the third day Brig. Collins, our much loved Commandant returned and ordered us to assemble in Chetwode Hall. We naturally wondered what his reactions would be.

He started by greeting us and said that he had learnt all that had happened in his absence and that he was happy to know that we had celebrated April Fools Day with such vigour. He was proud that the cadets had such initiative and spirit of adventure in celebrating it. April Fool was a custom to all. No single community could claim it to be its own. He was sorry that we had had to suffer for it. 'Your confinement to barracks is off', he said, and we heaved a sigh of relief. 'As a compensation for having lost your Sunday off, you will have this afternoon off. Be ready to go to town. Academy buses will be ready to take you at 3 o'clock this afternoon. Enjoy yourselves.'

What a grand chap he was! We all loved Brigadier Collins. He knew when a joke was a joke.

Note: This amusing anecdote was submitted by Lt Gen. Harbakhsh Singh a former Deputy Commandant for IMA.

Appendix III

The IMA Theatre

As there was no theatre at the IMA when I arrived, I decided to improvise one in one of the drill sheds near the Quartermaster's Store. The Cadets had as part of their English syllabus a book of one-act

The IMA Theatre.

Front row: Lt Col Thapan, 'Turk' Rahman, Brig. Baltrop, Mrs Mahadeo Singh, Field Marshal Lord Auchinleck, Mrs Parry, Admiral Parry

Second row: Maj. Iyappa, —, Lt Col Mahadeo Singh, —, Col Ayub Khan (later president of Pakistan), Mr Foot (Headmaster, Doon School, with pipe).

plays to study. Having studied these in class, the cadets taking parts in reading selected characters, I suggested that they should make an attempt to produce them on stage. They responded to this suggestion with enthusiasm. I then put it to them that they would have to give up some of their spare time rehearsing the plays to which they agreed.

I decided on each company choosing a play to produce at the end of term as a form of entertainment. They would have to choose their own cast, provide their own costumes and scenery and make the best use of the lighting available. At first the productions were pretty primitive, but the spirit was there, so I decided to make it a competition with a prize for the best production. Ernest Gould agreed that it would be a good idea, so preparations went ahead to entertain the Academy at the end of term. Fortunately the IMA had an army tailor who could be used to make costumes and an excellent Methods Office which would produce some scenery, and these I had permission to use.

When the time came I arranged for two nights, one for the junior officers and junior cadets and one for the Senior Officers, and the senior cadets, there being insufficient room to seat everyone in the old drill shed. The attendance was voluntary at first so we did not know what sort of audience to expect.

Ernest Gould decided he would attend the first night to give us some encouragement, and he was so impressed by the cadets ardour and initiative that he spoke to Brig. Baltrop the next morning suggesting that he should attend that night. We had advertised the productions on the notice boards starring Dreda Holman (who had kindly volunteered to take a female lead in one of the plays). As she was a senior officer's wife it attracted a good audience including the Commandant.

The following day Brig. Baltrop asked to see me and to congratulate me and all those cadets who had taken part. He was so pleased with the outcome that he informed me that he wished me to lay on a good play for the next Passing-out Parade, when the C-in-C would be present. He agreed that it was an excellent form of training and would become a regular feature.

Filled with enthusiasm and given permission to make full use of the military tailor, the Methods Office for scenery and the QM's Stores for props a suitable play had to be decided on. I decided upon *Arms and the Man*, a comedy with a military background. When the time came this was a resounding success, for in the vacation I gathered a team of officers and their wives to rehearse. At this time we had no

The IMA Players, 1948.

greenroom and had to use a tent at the back of the drill hall for the ladies. As a result of the success of *Arms and the Man*, we were given permission to construct a greenroom and a property room behind the stage by moving the stage forward and building a wall behind it to house the extension.

I had a board painted by the Methods Office to swing outside the drill hall like a pub sign with the simple words 'IMA Theatre'.

A review of *Arms and the Man* by Major James Wilson, the Adjutant is printed in Appendix V.

Appendix IV

The Amateur Dramatic Club

THE IMA PLAYERS have been very active this term both on and off the stage, i.e., organizing the new theatre, buying costumes, improving the lighting and acquiring property.

The first production was given in March, two performances being given on 20 and 24 March respectively. The production consisted of two plays one in Urdu, *Mamoo Jan*, and the other in English, *The Invisible Duke.*

Mamoo Jan, a comedy written and produced by A. Rahman of 'A' Company, showed that the Club has a talented author and producer as well as talented actors. The leading lights were A. Rahman as 'Mamoo Jan', T. C. Dharmani as 'The Dhobi', whose facial expressions were a delight to the audience; M. Jan as 'the Pathan', a very versatile actor, and F. Rahman Chaudhri, who portrayed various characters in different versions of this play, the best being his 'Subedar', which was a delight to watch.

Shafqat Syed not only gave us a memorable paniwala, but also, in collaboration with P. K. Roy, showed that the club has two first class make-up artists.

The Invisible Duke, by F. Sladen Smith starred Mrs Farhat Rahman as 'Lady Emelia', B. L. Hanna as 'the Astrologer' and G. D. Byrne as 'the Duke'. The two astrologer's assistants were ably portrayed by E. J. Elijah and A. Haq, and added much humour to the play. G. A. C. Manuel as 'Francisco' with a bristling moustache and wig of the same colour nearly succeeded in seducing 'Lady Emelia', with his buffoon's laugh, which she so convincingly told us was 'so exquisite' that made her swoon.

In April a revised version of *Mamoo Jan* was presented on the occasion of the C-in-C's visit. This proved very successful, and the additional scene, a schoolroom with real school children taking part and Janjua as the delightfully ignorant school inspector, made a most amusing finale.

The third production of *Mamoo Jan* was given at the Auchinleck Institute in May for the benefit of the Gurkha Units in Dehra Dun, and included an additional item, a dance by J. K. Kachari, which was skilfully performed.

Lastly four members of staff staged *The Clown of Stratford* by Sir John Squire. This was put on at a week's notice to be included in the music club concert in May.

Major Washtell as 'Shaxpur' showed us convincingly that 'the immortal bard' might have been a clever blackmailer but above all that he was an accomplished actor, even if he was found 'a poor man doing walking-on parts'.

Francis Bacon, Lord Verulam (Lt Col Gould) gave us inspired moments as a poet and as a hen-pecked husband, while Lady Verulam (Mrs Hilda Washtell), in a charming half moon Elizabethan hat with wimple, gave us a convincing portrayal of a devoted but managing wife. Her performance revealed to us her acting ability and her great skill as a dress designer. The servant portrayed by Major Wright brought the play to end with the announcement of 'Shaxpur's' death, and the revelation (to Lord Verulam) that he (the servant not Major Wright) was really Ben Jonson.

It is hoped that by the beginning of next term the two new green rooms and store rooms will be completed. This will greatly add to the club's opportunities of producing full length plays in the future.

Most Companies in their end of term concerts included skits, farces and playlets, all of which encourage the present dramatic club to believe that there is an even greater abundance of histrionic talent available for bigger ventures next term, including Shaw's *Arms and the Man.*

Appendix V

Arms and the Man

G. B. Shaw

Arms and the Man was a particularly suitable choice to play to a military audience at an institution like the IMA. The problems which beset a 'Chocolate cream soldier' are familiar to all regular officers and could be relied on to appeal to regular officer aspirants as well. To an excellent choice of play was added a standard of production, scenery, decor and

Arms and the Man

Left to right: A.C. Byrne (Nicola); Pat Reynolds (Louka), Don Washtell (Bluntschli), Jean Harley (Raina), David Harley (Officer), YDA Beale (Mrs Petkoff)

Seated: Peter Gorb (Saranoff), Charles Wright (Major Petkoff)

acting which was of a totally different class to anything previously seen at the IMA. Consequently, a visit to the IMA theatre on Tuesday 9 September proved an experience which was as pleasant as it was refreshing.

The outstanding individual performance was undoubtedly Major D. G. Washtell as Captain Bluntschli – equally convincing in a Lady's Bedchamber or in planning the move of two divisions in a drawing room. He gave a remarkably polished performance. He was well supported by Major Wright as Petkoff and Captain Gorb as Saranoff. Major Wright's dress, appearance and manner qualified him for permanent membership of the Cheltenham and District Golf Club while Captain Gorb made the most of Saranoff's outrageous quixotry. The all-important female parts were filled equally admirably. Mrs Harley gave a delightful performance as Raina and brought out to the full the way in which a romantic schoolgirl can be changed by the force of events into a woman of the world. Mrs Beal as Catherine gave a splendid supporting performance, while Miss Reynolds made an admirably pert Louisa. Byrne as Nicola made the most of his past as a servant who knows his station and at the same time how to get the best out of his employers.

But it was as a cohesive effort that this production of *Arms and the Man* impressed me most. From the moment that the curtain went up until the end of the play the cast acted as if they were a real company and not a mere collection of Amateur Actors. The admirable precision of the acting and production, coupled with the very high standard of decor, took one right out of the IMA and on to the London stage. *Arms and the Man* was a production which will not quickly be forgotten.

A. J. W.

Appendix VI

The Transformation of the Theatre

WE CAN NOW BOAST OF A REAL THEATRE, for during this term a complete transformation has taken place. The days of the old PT shed are over, the PT Staff have moved their office and equipment elsewhere.

The notable changes are the raising of the floor in tiers, the building

Cast of *The Scheming Lieutenant.*

of a back wall and an addition of three rooms at the back, including a ladies' room and lavatories, a soft drink bar, an orchestral pit, and last by no means least a new proscenium and scenery and new curtaining throughout the Theatre. There is also a sunken model in the centre of the hall for instructional use. This is covered over when not in use.

For these improvements we are indebted to the Commandant and Deputy Commandant for sanctioning these improvements and supplying the funds; to Major D. M. Kee for the planning and executing of the work, in record time, on the proscenium and for the magnificent new lighting; and to Major H. R. H. Daniell for curtaining the hall and improving the green rooms.

We now require permanent seating in the hall and an additional green room. It is hoped that 1950 will see these additions made.

Appendix VII

Down to the Tons Valley in December

IF YOU ARE ABLE TO DISSOCIATE the Tons Valley from thoughts of arduous Field Training, it is an area both beautiful and full of interest for those who take any pleasure in Natural History. Every month of the year brings a change of character in appearance, fauna and flora, and to the close observer almost every day of every month.

Suppose that it is mid-December and we walk down to the valley. Before descending, a good look across it is well worth while. The flat foreground dotted with large Pepal trees, the boulder-strewn river beds, intersected first by more or less parallel ranges of hills about the same height as we are above the valley, with scrub jungle-covered slopes, then more ranges steadily rising clothed with sal forest up to the mountains. To the west the furthest and highest mountain tops visible are snow-capped, also if there has been a spell of bad weather those east of Mussoorie. The mountains are hazy with not much colour in the early afternoon.

As the valley lies about 170 feet below the IMA building, we take one of the many paths that lead down the cliff through thick scrub jungles. There is so much to notice about this charming strip of jungle with its bridle path that runs the whole length of the cliff from the old CI camp to the end of the Forest Research bungalows, except for two or three breaks. First the greenery. A few groups of Sal trees, an odd Pepal and some Shisham. The rest are shrubs and small trees. As the Research Institute is close by, and they are so helpful in supplying those who wish to know, with the names of any plants they like to ask about, it is a simple matter to find out, and as well to remember the Latin names for future reference besides the local ones.

Among the shrubs at present Holmskioldia Sanguinea (Cup & Saucer plant) with long sprays of tawny red flowers attracts attention. A few white blossoms of Pyrus Pashia are out. In early spring it will be out in masses. Mallotus Philippinensis is the most common shrub, its spikes of fruit later on are covered with a red powder from which dyes are made and used in Hindu religious ceremonies, the fruit now is just beginning to form. Prickly bushes of Carissa Opaca (Corunda), also very common, have ripening berries, which when quite black are delicious eating. It would take too long to talk of all the plants, but each one has at its appointed time of year to come into prominence by reason of its flowers or fruit.

The slope of this cliff is not even; it is broken by many ravines. The banks of the ravines and the bridle path are mostly moss-covered with varieties of ferns growing out of them. Here and there along them there are large round holes, the nest holes in summer of those handsome birds, the Blue-bearded Bee-eater and White-breasted Kingfisher.

Of insect life there is little to be seen, it is now too cold. Most are hibernating, each in its own fashion. But place a white sheet below the overhanging branches of a shrub, shake those branches vigorously and the examine the 'catch'. Very soon among the dead leaves and twigs, tiny and often grotesquely-shaped forms of life will begin to move. To us, the highest form of animal life, all other forms of life should be worth our notice. We reflect on the thousands of kinds of insects not visible now, that will begin again their life cycle with the Spring.

From the gardens of the bungalows above us come shouts from the malis in their attempts to drive away the marauding bands of monkeys. Destructive they are, but it is so amusing to watch their antics and human behaviour. Things are getting noisy, there are excited yelps from the dogs who have come with us, a startled movement from a bush nearby, an upward leap and a flash of a white tail, the hare is off with the dogs in hot pursuit. These dogs are not at all likely to catch their quarry, but a good time is had by all during the chase. Some other rodent or a Jackal or Civet Cat is just as likely to be the quarry.

Now from the depths of a ravine comes a raucous chorus of 'laughter', which might almost be described as part singing. It is the Himalayan White-crested Laughing Thrushes. Probably one or two will come into view, the leader crouching over a horizontal branch urging on the rest of his band below, splendid with his shining white-crested head, and neck, which is broken only by a broad black line through the eye, the rest of the plumage being sober brown. They are residents of these ravines. They have sounded the alarm for all. With a whir of wings and shrill cries a flock of Slaty-headed Parakeets rise from a group of Shisham trees, where they have been cracking open the pods to eat the seeds. As they fly the bright yellow tips of the tail feathers are plainly visible and differentiate them from the other parakeets that are here as residents. They are the Parakeets of the hills and are only here for the winter, like so many other species of birds about this strip of jungle and the valley. Another whir, but of heavier wings. A jungle cock crosses high above the path to cover above. The sun catches his bright hackle feathers and his ladies scatter in all directions, No, don't clutch for your gun, they are our IMA pets, unique in the almost tame way they will sometimes come into our gardens to feed, and it would be a poor thing to destroy or scare them away. A long shrill whistle and a black bird with an orange bill flies up from a ravine and away – the Himalayan Whistling Thrush, also here only for the winter. We can hear him in the early mornings and late evenings singing a clear beautiful song.

With airy independence from tree-top to tree-top move the scarlet and black male Short-billed Minivets with their yellow and grey females. A party of White-cheeked Bulbuls, which have a punch-like crest and a tuft of yellow feathers under the tail, are not scared as they continue their feast of Pepal fruit, only increasing their merry calls and lively behaviour. Also not scared but moving rather more quickly from tree to tree is a 'mixed hunting association' of small insectivorous birds. There are many different species among them, some resident, some only winter visitors, each species behaving in its special fashion, but all must have discovered that in hunting together the maximum amount of food is obtainable. Six or seven Grey Hornbills leave the Pepal tree where they too have been feasting with a few flaps of the wings and a long glide. They are clumsy but amusing. Quite unconcerned from high up in a tree the Green Barbet starts its monotonous 'Kutur-kutur-kutur', but only a few sequences of it at this time of year. From some distance the Tree Pie and Jungle Babblers seem to be blaming each other for the disturbances by seeing who can scold the loudest. To get a good view of the shy Flycatchers, Petal-peckers, Sunbirds and Babblers that inhabit this strip of jungle takes time and much patience.

At the foot of the cliff we leave the jungle and are on the comparatively bare valley. The trees along the edge of the cliff jungles are bare except for small bunches of seeds, which the Grey Tits are now performing acrobatics to get at. Last month the leaves of these trees were a glory of red and gold autumnal tints. It is Sapium Sebifarum, the Chinese Tallow Tree, as the name implies. In China candles are made from the oil from the seeds. The short shrub also Adhatoda Vasica grows everywhere along the edge of the jungle. In early spring it will blossom out with white flowers lasting for months.

Crossing this plain that borders the river beds has its own interest. The dogs, hot from the chase in the jungles, plunge into the much reduced stagnant pools used by the cattle for drinking and turn their attention to catching the frogs as they leap here and there. Almost the only trees here are Pepals, which are now almost bare of leaves. Again we know that each supports a variety of hidden life. A querulous chatter and the face of a Spotted Owlet stares out of a hole in one of them. There is probably a whole family of them living there. The dry black pods of Cassia tora, one of the commonest of weeds, rattle as we walk through a patch of it. Accompanying the scattered herd and grazing cattle are a flock of Yellow Wagtails, which take full advantage of the insects, etc. that are disturbed by the animals. The amount of yellow in their plumage varies greatly, some with scarcely a trace of it.

If we continue our walk across the valley and back we can pass through the different types of country, the rivers that have only a few clear streams running between the boulders, the pieces of stone waste-land between them covered by thorny Ziziphus (Ber) with their bright red plums, so attractive to humans and birds alike. Cultivated fields of young wheat and chunnar form a green haze. Other fields, which are being prepared for sowing, are irrigated by water drawn off in channels from the rivers. Each of these types have their special set of birds, which are residents or visitors to them.

The peoples of the valley are as pleasant as everything else in it. The children request peeps through our field-glasses instead of only the usual 'baksheesh'. Near the two or three small villages the people will probably ask us to partake of some hospitality in their houses, which unfortunately we shall have to refuse if we are to be home by dusk. Time is far too short and winter evenings close so quickly.

When we have retraced our steps or taken one of the many other ways back, the mountains are no longer colourless. The setting sun transforms the haze about them into colours that any painter or poet would revel in his art to set down. For us, who perhaps have no such ability, it is just the thought of how wonderful everything really is. We have seen and heard and felt only an infinitesimal part of what is there waiting for us to discover.

Dulcie Wright

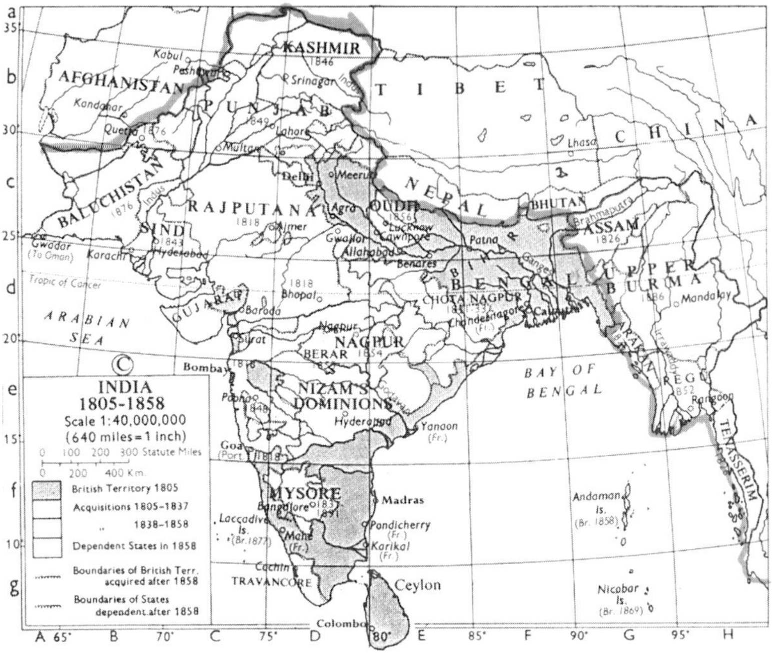

India before Partition.

India after Partition.

Appendix VIII

A Tribute to Jack Gibson

JACK GIBSON, who was the first Principal of the National Defence Academy Interservice Wing came out to India in 1937 to join the staff of the newly opened Doon School in Dehra Dun, of which Mr Foot was the first Principal. He had been a master at Harrow for some years.

He was loaned to the NDA and remained in the post until the NDA moved to Karakawasla near Poona. Not only was Jack a devoted educationist, but also a good skier, trekker, canoeist and mountaineer, being Chairman of the Himalayan Club from 1970–73. Ten Singh, who later climbed Mount Everest successfully, was at one time one of his sherpas.

On leaving the NDA, he returned to the Doon School as Principal and later became Principal of Mayo College, Ajmer, where he ultimately retired. Here he wrote his autobiography, *India As I Saw It*, giving a vivid picture of his life in the form of letters which he wrote home. His life was devoted to education and above all to his students, who included the Maharajah of Jaipur.

Jack was educated at Haileybury College and Sydney Sussex, Cambridge, where he read English and History and captained the University Fencing Team. He was awarded the OBE for his services to education by the British Government and the Padma Shri by the Indian Government.

A Gibson Room has been set up in the Mayo College Museum exhibiting his skiing and trekking material, his purse, his typewriters, articles of his clothing and furniture and even his pipe.

He was a much loved teacher and friend and I am informed that a postage stamp is to be issued to commemorate his life of devotion to education in India.

The NDA Interservice Wing was indeed fortunate to have Jack Gibson as its first Principal, and we his contemporaries were fortunate to have him as a friend.

C. W.

Appendix IX

Wildlife at the IMA

THE IMA IS SITUATED SOME 2,000 ft above sea level on a plateau above the Tons Valley with scrub jungle at the foot of the officers' bungalows, where numerous wild creatures are to be found (see *Down to the Tons Valley in December*). Some of these wild creatures invaded the IMA grounds by night, the most common of which was the jackal. They were seldom seen but often heard.

One night while cycling back from some IMA function, a whole pack of jackals raged through my front garden nearly colliding with my cycle in the dark. On another occasion while cycling home after a Bridge competition (Officers versus Cadets) I saw what I thought was a very large dog scratching itself on a corner of the playing fields. I had no cycle lamp so I shone my torch on it as I passed within 20 yards of it. I concluded that it was much too large to be a dog or jackal, so I switched off my torch and cycled on hurriedly to my bungalow nearby. A few minutes later while I was undressing I heard a shot ring out. The next morning I asked the Commandant whether he had heard the shot. He replied that as he drove his car into his drive he saw a panther, went indoors, loaded his rifle and shot the panther in his garden. I had been wise not to confirm my suspicions that night.

It was quite a common sight to see flying foxes electrocuted on the live wires outside our bungalows. Their bodies resemble small foxes and their wings those of a large bat.

One evening I heard a frantic noise in my back garden. Looking out of a window I saw a python trying to swallow a large toad, which was creating mayhem. Within seconds three of our red setters were setting about the python, which disgorged the unfortunate toad that in no time leapt back into the mali pond. The servants then came running from their quarters with sticks and stones shouting and screaming.

Whenever the python lunged towards one dog, the other two attacked it from their vantage points. I was afraid for the safety of the dogs, but they were fearless, harrying the python from all sides. One of the servants heaved a brick at the python hitting it squarely in the neck, whereupon it turned and fled into the bushes. It must have been about ten foot long for it had risen to a height of five or six feet when it was struck.

In no time it had disappeared into the next compound pursued by the dogs. I was very worried because my wife was out in the Tons valley with one of our dogs and it was growing dark. The servants came running out with hurricane battis to search for it and drive it away, knowing that my wife would be returning by that route. Fortunately she had taken the precaution to return by the Forest Research Institute gate and arrived unaware of the danger, having once disturbed a nest of krites in the semi-jungle below our garden.

Our saddest experience was when one of our red setters set upon its own mother as we started upon our evening walk. We were naturally very worried and hurried back and isolated the dog and phoned for the Dehra Dun vet, who motored in immediately. He tested the dog with a stick which it bit fiercely. Then he offered it water which it would not drink. These were sure signs of dumb rabies, so we had to have the dog put down. Unfortunately for us we had to undergo the full anti-rabic treatment of daily stomach injections every day for the next two weeks. Needless to say we did not start barking or biting our friends.

To end on a pleasant note, no one can ever forget the brain fever bird that keeps one awake at night in the hot weather. There was one that screamed up the tonic scale and then down again, crying, 'Listen, listen, listen, listen', ever louder and then, 'Did you hear me, did you hear me, did you hear me, did you hear me,' four times, and then after a pause it repeated the double refrain, until it drove you silly.

The other brain fever bird which was just as infuriating, seemed to say over and over again 'Lost your rifle, lost your rifle, lost your rifle' three times, pausing momentarily before repeating the cadet's nightmare, 'Lost your rifle, lost your rifle, lost your rifle'. It certainly succeeded in keeping officer and cadet alike awake night after night, night after night, night after night.

C. W.

Appendix X

A Visit to Kashmir

BEFORE I LEFT INDIA, I had a surprise letter form Gen. Mahadeo Singh asking me and my wife to escort his wife, Sheila, and his two children to Kashmir, where he had taken over form Gen. Thimayya, who in turn took over from him at the IMA.

Kashmir at that time, just after the Kashmir War, was still a non-family station, but now Mahadeo Singh had decided to relax the rule and allow officers' wives to be accommodated once more.

Not having been to Kashmir before we were delighted to accept his invitation and agreed to go during the summer recess. As British Officers were not yet allowed to visit Kashmir, Mahadeo told me that I must travel as a civilian and that he would provide us with passes to enter Kashmir.

We had to travel by train to Jammu, where we would stay with the general commanding that area and travel on the next day by air. We duly arrived and were welcomed by the GOC and accommodated in his house.

It so happened that one of the former IMA officers was commanding a regiment there and we were asked out for drinks that evening. I had changed the clothes in which I had been travelling and had left our passes in a coat in our bedroom. What was my consternation the next morning when I discovered that my pass and my wife's were missing, but the other passes were still there. At the breakfast table I informed my host what had happened. He told us not to worry and that he would accompany us to the plane and that we would be met by Mahadeo on arrival. So all seemed well.

The air passage was very bumpy and first the children and then Sheila were sick so my wife was able to minister to them until we arrived.

I decided to get off last as we had no passes and thought that as we were travelling with the General's wife, we would go through unchallenged, but that was not to be. A security officer asked me for our passes and when I said I had none, he politely asked us to follow him. In the meantime Mahadeo was greeting his family and they had walked to the staff car. When Mahadeo saw us walking in the opposite direction he shouted, 'Charles, where are you going?' I replied 'I've just been arrested, sir.'

'Don't be such a bloody fool', he shouted to the unfortunate security officer, 'He's my guest'. So I was released from custody and we accompanied Mahadeo and his family in his station waggon to Flag Staff House, where we were to spend the night. Here we were told he was giving a special reception for Sheila and ourselves, and that he would take us to our houseboat, where we were to spend the next ten days, the following morning.

The party was a great success. I had explained that our passes had been stolen and that we would require new passes in order to leave the country.

'Don't worry, old boy,' he said 'I'll fix it.'

So the next morning he and Sheila accompanied us to the Dahl Lake and showed us our delightful houseboat, which had every comfort – sitting room, dining room, two bedrooms with bathrooms and a servants' boat and kitchen alongside all powered by electricity. There was also a 'shikara' to enable us to travel about the lake, the houseboat being moored to the land and connected to an electric pylon.

Needless to say we had a wonderful holiday, Mahadeo and Sheila taking us out to various places of interest, including the Shalimar Gardens and a wonderful day's outing visiting a glacier. On our own we went for wonderful walks, water-skied, bathed and sunbathed. We also paid several visits to Srinagar, where we bought numerous souvenirs, including a nest of Kashmir tables, a standard lamp, a model houseboat and a Cashmere shawl, all of which we have to this very day.

When our time was up, Mahadeo invited us to spend the last night with him. There was to be a special farewell party to round off our holiday. During the party I reminded him that we needed our passes to get out of the country by road. He had quite forgotten and called his unfortunate Adjutant, and gave him orders to get our passes as we were leaving early the next morning. The poor fellow left the party and was not seen again until the next morning, when he provided us with civilian passes. My pass was made out for a Mr Charles Henry

Edmund (my three first names) and wife, but no surname. So officially Charles Wright and wife never visited Kashmir at all.

However all went well and we caught the civilian bus which travelled over the Hump and down the winding mountainside with its spectacular views, never to be forgotten.

Soon after we had left Srinagar all civilian traffic was halted because an army convoy was approaching, so my wife and I got out to have a breather. Suddenly we heard shouts and yells from one of the open trucks and we were greeted with salutes and laughter, for it contained a batch of ex-cadets from the IMA, all young officers now.

What a splendid farewell from our newly-commissioned officers. It was a day to remember.

C. W.

Indian types sketched by the author

Urdu Class

About the Author

CHARLES WRIGHT was born in Pachmarhi, India, the son of a senior Police Officer. He was educated at Clifton College, King's College, London, and at Downing College, Cambridge, where he studied under Dr F. R. Leavis.

On graduation he went to India and taught in two Military Schools

The author and his wife with Senior IMA Officers and their wives in 1988.

before the war. On the outbreak of war he had the unique distinction of calling himself up.

During the war he served in the Royal Corps of Signals as a cipher officer in Persia, Iraq and Egypt before returning to India in 1944, when he transferred to the Army Education Corps, whose centre was in Pachmarhi, his birthplace.

Before being posted to the Indian Military Academy, he commanded the Eastern Command Educational Training Centre in Shillong, Assam. At the IMA he served under the last British Commandant, Brig. A. B. Baltrop, and the first Indian Commandant, Brig. (later General) Thakur Mahadeo Singh, and finally under General Thimayya, who later became Chief of Staff and United Nations Representative, first in Korea and later in Cyprus, where Jim Wilson served under him.

Now a free lance journalist the author has published a brief social history of Porlock, where he now lives, with his wife Vera, whose encouragement and support in publishing this tribute to the IMA has been an inspiration, without which this book might have never been written.

The author in uniform